Living With Autism

Sammie's Story

By Suzanne C. Brown

authorHOUSE®

AuthorHouse™
1663 Liberty Drive
Bloomington, IN 47403
www.authorhouse.com
Phone: 1-800-839-8640

First published by AuthorHouse 12/14/2010

ISBN: 978-1-4567-1940-1 (e)
ISBN: 978-1-4567-1941-8 (sc)

Library of Congress Control Number: 2010918772

Printed in the United States of America

TABLE OF CONTENTS

PART ONE

PART TWO

PART THREE

INTRODUCTION

Her name is Samantha Jo Brown and she is autistic. She was born in 1971, a time when very little was known about autism. Most people, including me, her mother, had never even heard the word autistic. This is a true story about a beautiful little girl growing up in a world that she does not understand.

Our journey into an unknown world began with a chance meeting of a family member's pet, of all things. Little did I ever imagine that, when my husband's aunt and uncle stopped by for an unannounced visit, our lives would be influenced forever by an invisible force.

Samantha was my fourth baby and born when my other children were in their early teens. She was a very welcome addition to the family and was the picture of health and beauty. Family members stopped by to welcome our new addition and I felt as proud as could be. Experience with my first three babies had created a wealth of knowledge concerning children, their health and development.

Our family was happy and our home was a welcome place for visitors. But, my motherly feelings went on alert when my husband's uncle, aunt, their son and his pet monkey arrived at the door.

This was the beginning of a change in our lives that brought doubt, uncertainty, and a totally unknown area of limitations, known as autism.

Samantha never fully developed the ability to speak and we were told early on by speech therapists that she probably never would. Consequently, she carried journals with her throughout her school years. I wrote to the teachers and caregivers and they responded. This book is compiled from those journals.

PROLOGUE

She is lying in a hospital crib with tubes and needles providing sustenance and medication to her tiny body. The sign on her door says "ISOLATION" and it strikes terror to my heart. The doctors and nurses are grim-faced and unsmiling. They are trying to save her life. Covered with a hospital gown, gloves and mask, I can only look at Sammie, I can't touch my baby. She has been here for less than a week, but has already had two spinal taps. She squirms and throws her arms up and the needles make her hands bleed, so the nurse moves them to another location. When that one tears her little hand open, they move it down to her foot.

CHAPTER ONE

Samantha

On the morning of the 21ˢᵗ of April 1971, Samantha Jo Brown was born with very little fuss. It was a natural childbirth, no anesthetic, after about five hours of labor. She weighed 9 pounds and 5 ounces. She was the perfect picture of health and my husband Roy and I bonded with her, loved her, and were anxious to get her home. When she was four days old, we took her out to the farm where my mother was waiting for us. She had been helping her grandchildren hold down the fort while I was in the hospital.

In the following days, Roy's family began stopping by to see our new pride and joy. His uncle and aunt, Paul and Anna Roberts; his sisters, Shannon and Tammy and their husbands, all from his mother's side of the family.

Samantha was about 3 weeks old when his uncle and aunt from his father's side arrived. I had not met them before then. He was a big, beefy looking man and she was a short woman who was about as wide as she was tall. Neither of them looked like they bathed very often. They had brought their teen-age son with them and he was holding a small monkey in his arms. I was appalled that they had brought this nasty looking wild creature into our house. I was not very cordial to them and they didn't stay very long. Little did I know that the monkey would change Samantha's and my lives forever, as you will find out later in our story.

About four days later, Samantha stopped drinking her bottle. She was restless and fussy all day and I couldn't get her to drink her formula. She is my fourth baby, so I am an experienced mother and I wasn't too worried. When I took her temperature, the thermometer only registered

99 degrees. No other symptoms had presented themselves, but as I held her in my arms and looked at her eyes I could see that she was in pain. When I put her in her crib that night, I had the terrible feeling that she might not wake up in the morning. Since it was a weekend and my pediatrician was out of town I knew I couldn't call him. In the morning I drove her the 20 miles into town to the Emergency Room at the closest hospital. The doctor who examined her and listened to my description of her symptoms said: "She might have a little cold, but it isn't serious. You appear to be just another nervous mother." He sent us back home.

The following morning her temperature was still hovering around 99 degrees, but suddenly she had a convulsion. Her body stiffened, then her back arched, her hands flailed and her eyes rolled up and became unfocused. I telephoned Dr. Connor who had seen her in the ER. His response was, "It isn't unusual for babies to have a convulsion when they have a cold". She suffered numerous convulsions throughout that day. I called Dr. Connor again because I was sure the seizures were very serious and I wanted her admitted to the hospital. He was unmoved. After all, I was "just a nervous mother".

The next day was Monday and Dr. Hollis, my pediatrician, was back in town. When I took her to him and he examined her, she still just had that low-grade fever and he was inclined to agree with the ER doctor. He was about to send us back home when she suddenly had another convulsion. He looked startled and said, "I believe we should have my colleague (Dr. so-and-so, I was too upset to hear his name) take a look at her." Finally I was being taken seriously and she was being admitted to the hospital!

Dr. Hollis met me at the Admissions Desk and took Sammie from my arms. He said, "You stay here and start filling out forms. I will come back to talk to you as soon as we have some definitive answers."

I don't really know how long it was before he reappeared, but it felt like an eternity. I was terribly distraught, trying not to let my tears fall, and praying to God. I said the same thing over and over "Dear God, please don't let her die! Please let her live and I promise that I will take care of her and love her always no matter what kind of problems she has!" I was thinking that perhaps she had cerebral palsy or something similar.

He sat down beside me, picked up my hand and said. "We think

Samantha has viral meningitis. I will take you to see her, but you will have to "gown up" because it is very contagious at this point. Also, you will only be able to stay a few minutes because the doctors and nurses need to be able to work on her."

I was trembling so hard that a nurse had to help me with the gown, mask and gloves. When I got into the room, there was a flurry of activity by people in white gowns and I could immediately see that I was in the way and could do nothing for my baby. I turned and stumbled out the door and was almost immediately enfolded in my mother's arms. I had telephoned her while I was in the waiting room and she had just gotten to the hospital. She said, 'Oh, Sue, are you all right? I have been so worried about you!"

I suddenly realized that I was her baby and she truly was as concerned for me as I was for the little one I was leaving behind in the hospital room.

CHAPTER TWO

July 1970 – Lowell, Michigan

As the Executive Secretary to the District Manager of Shell Oil Company, I was the liaison for the 33 salesmen scattered around the state. Mr. Lester demanded complete control of the sales force, so I had to know where they were and how to contact them. I also had to contact all of the local service stations when there was a price change for gasoline. I had had this job for five years and I loved it.

I worked in Grand Rapids, Michigan, but I lived 15 miles out of town. I was a single mother with three teenage children, two girls and a boy. Their ages were 17, 16, and 14. I had recently moved them from Grand Rapids to a 20 acre farm in Lowell. Our farmhouse was somewhere between 75 and 100 years old, a big two-story house with 4 bedrooms upstairs and one downstairs. There was also a big old barn (so old that it had wood pegs holding it together instead of nails) and several other outbuildings.

As I left the office, my mind was occupied with details about the workday. I needed to make travel arrangements for Mr. Lester to travel to Shell Headquarters in Chicago. When I was almost halfway home, my mind left the office behind and focused on the kids. This switch happened every day. It was as if I had two very separate lives, one in town and the other in the country. We all had assigned chores and I wondered if the girls (Karen and Laura) had finished washing and drying the morning's dishes and had Larry fed the dogs and the two pet goats? I know for certain that Laura has fed the two horses and maybe already has them saddled, ready for the two of us to go for a quick ride. And, let's see, what do I have on hand for tonight's dinner?

On Saturday morning my ex-husband picks up the kids. He lives on the North side of Grand Rapids with his second wife. He always complains bitterly about having to make the 40 mile round trip to get them and I can see that he has a scowl on his face. I feel sorry for the kids who have to go with him whether they want to or not. He will return them early Sunday afternoon, so I am now alone for the weekend.

My morning is occupied with the usual housecleaning, laundry and so forth, but time is dragging without the kids. It is early July, so I know there will be a baseball game at the park in Ada. Ada is the little village I grew up in and it is located halfway between Lowell and Grand Rapids. I went to school with about half the guys on the team and still stay in touch with them and their wives and kids. They call their team "The Orphans" because they don't have a sponsor.

The game was just starting when I got there so I was standing on the sidelines beside the bleachers. Suddenly I noticed a tall, dark handsome man who has evidently just struck out and is returning to the bleachers. I do not know who he is, but I think, "Wow! Is he good-looking!" At that same moment, he noticed me. I smiled at him and he smiled at me. He came over and said. "Hi! I'm Roy Brown. Who are you?" I told him my name was Sue Gray. We both laughed over the "colors" of our names and spent the rest of the afternoon half watching the game and getting acquainted.

He is there with his sister and brother-in-law, Tammy and David. I went to grade school in Ada with David. When the game ended, most of the participants were planning to go to "The Dirty Shame" for beer and pizza. There were two taverns in Ada; one was called the Lena Lou and the other was the Dirty Shame. Tammy and Dave invited me to go with them, but I had to get back home to take care of all of our animals. Roy asked for my phone number before I left.

He called early the next morning. Sunday and the kids would still be gone until mid-afternoon. It would be so nice to have some company instead of facing another lonely day. He arrived in a big, old, beat up Oldsmobile that looked like a tank. We ended up driving North of Lowell on a winding road that followed the Grand River. He was telling me about his family. He had sustained many losses – his father had been killed in a tree-trimming accident, his mother had remarried and then had been beaten to death by her new husband, and Roy's wife had left him for another man. He was lonelier than I was!

We ended up at the home of another sister, Shannon, who had nine month old twin daughters, and a big smiling husband named Joe. They were delighted to see Roy who apparently had not been around to visit for a while.

We got back to the farm just as my three were returning. After giving me hugs, they greeted Roy cautiously, wondering what was going on. They were not accustomed to finding strange men hanging around. We all did the barn chores together. Roy was introduced to the horses, dogs, and goats and obviously enjoyed them. After dinner, we settled in our big dining room for a rousing, competitive game of cards. Roy was completely at ease and it began to feel like he belonged.

After that he was there every evening when I got home from work and it was not long before he was staying through the night. He had quite a large extended family living in Greenville, another small town about 40 miles North of Lowell. In the evenings we often drove around visiting in the homes of various aunts, uncles, and cousins. We also liked to go to a tavern in Lowell called "The Riverside". They had a large dance floor and a small group that played western music.

One evening we were drinking beer and dancing and the band was about to take a break. Roy got up from our table and went to talk to them. They smiled and nodded their heads at whatever he was saying. I assumed he was making a request for a song. When the band returned, I was astonished when the leader said, "We have a guest singer with us tonight, folks. Roy, come on up here." Roy picked up the microphone and belted out a surprisingly good imitation of George Jones singing "White Lightning", a novelty song about "Pappy's corn likker". The crowd loved it and several of them bought him shots of whiskey that he slugged down.

He was obviously getting drunk and I decided it was time for us to go home. He insisted that he was OK to drive and we only had four miles of country road, so I got into the passenger seat. He didn't say a word, but he hunched over the steering wheel with a dark black scowl on his face. When he stopped the car in our driveway, I started to open the passenger door. Suddenly he grabbed my arm, dragged me out the driver's side door, and roughly shoved me up against the car. He got in my face and shouted, "DON'T EVER EMBARRASS ME LIKE THAT AGAIN!" I was terribly frightened and knew I was dealing with a mad man! I managed to jerk away from him and ran for the front door. He was right on my heels and I slammed the door in his face. As I was turning the lock, he put his fist right through the window. A shard of glass hit the corner of my eye. It hurt like the dickens and started bleeding. When he realized what he had done, all the fight went out of him and he was instantly back to the man I thought I knew and had even thought that I loved. He was sorry, he was so contrite; he ran cold water on his handkerchief and gently bathed the cut. He begged me to forgive him; he promised it would never happen again. He even blamed it on the fact that he had some Indian blood and, therefore, could not tolerate hard liquor. He didn't know that when that window shattered, all of my feeling for him was shattered with it. I screamed at him, "Get out! Get out of my house! Get out of my life! Don't ever come back here or I will have you thrown in jail!" He left and I heard his car going down the driveway. He didn't come back and he didn't telephone.

Two weeks later, I realized I was pregnant.

Oh, God, what was I going to do? Abortion was illegal in Michigan then. I was horrified, embarrassed, frightened, panicked! So I did what I always did when I was in trouble, I went to see my Mom. She listened quietly while I cried my way through my explanation of what had happened. Finally she said, "Sue, do you remember what you said when Karen, your firstborn, was placed in your arms?"

"Yes", I said, "now I will never be alone again." I never knew where that thought came from, but there it was.

Mom said, "Your children will soon be all grown up and gone. Do you suppose God has sent you this baby to keep you from being alone again?"

My Mom! No recriminations, no lectures. Simple acceptance. I hugged her and started back to the farm knowing what I had to do. I would be driving past The Dirty Shame on my way home and it was a weekend so I stopped on the off-chance that Roy might be there. He wasn't, but Shannon and Dave were. They, of course, knew that things had ended badly with Roy and me. I sat down with them and told them I was pregnant with Roy's child. Then, to my embarrassment, I started weeping again. I stood up, left the tavern, and drove on home.

Roy showed up at the farm less than two hours later. He said, "I would be so honored if you would be the mother of my children. I love you. Please marry me!"

I said, "Alright, I will marry you, but here's what I want you to promise me. I want you to pledge that you will stay away from hard liquor since you don't seem to be able to handle it. And I want a second baby as soon as possible after this one is born because I don't want to raise an only child. And I want you to stick around for at least 17 years to help me raise your children."

He eagerly agreed to each point and solemnly promised that he would not fail me.

He was elated. "I am so glad you have forgiven me!"

"Oh, I have forgiven you, but I haven't forgotten! If you EVER lay a hand on me again, you will be in jail before you can say 1-2-3!"

In order to understand what would motivate two people to enter into such a cold sounding unromantic agreement, you would have to understand that we were brought up in small, rural towns in a time when abortion was unknown (or at least never discussed) and marriage followed pregnancy like day followed night. There were plenty of babies born "early" but none that we knew of were ever born without the benefit of marriage. In those days, divorce was barely tolerated and illegitimate children simply did not exist in polite society. Even though the 1970's were the beginning of women's liberation, small town country folk were still clinging to a strict code of morality.

The following day Shannon and Dave accompanied us to a small church in Lowell and witnessed our marriage. That was in August and our Samantha was going to be born in April.

Roy got a job in a small shop that polished and buffed chrome automobile parts. He was paid by the piece and seemed to be good at his work. I was too embarrassed for my friends at Shell Oil to know that I was pregnant so I resigned. With what I had paid into the retirement fund, along with matching funds from the company, I had a moderate savings account. I planned to get another job as soon as the baby was old enough to go to childcare.

My children were never aware of the violence that Roy had exhibited and I had covered it up with a completely false story about an automobile accident. I told them I had been injured when we had been struck by another car and the car window was shattered. His relationship with them continued as it had started with him helping with the care of the animals and joining in with card games or whatever we chose to do in the evenings.

Karen, my 17 year old, had completed driver's education and had her license. She was delighted that I was staying home because I was no longer using my car. However, the rule was that, if she wanted to use my car, she had to buy gasoline for it. There was a small country diner called Jimmy's Grill about a half mile from our farm and she got a job there as a waitress. Her goal was to save enough money to buy a car of her own. When she started bringing home a salary and tips, Laura, my 16 year old, followed her example and also went to work at Jimmy's. Before the winter was over, Larry, my 14 year old son, joined them at Jimmy's as a dishwasher and busboy. Mother was right—my children would soon be "leaving the nest".

Roy and I had been married for nearly a year when Samantha became ill. It was late afternoon when I left the hospital and drove back to our farm. Now, as I walked into our farmhouse, he was sitting on the sofa in the livingroom and he had obviously had several bottles of beer. The expression on his face was dark, stormy, with his black eyebrows drawn into a frown.

"How is the baby?" he said, as he raised the beer bottle he was holding and took another drink.

"She is terribly ill. She's in isolation because they think it is viral meningitis". I could barely get the words out past the lump in my throat. "But why didn't you come to town after you finished work? I expected to see you at the hospital."

"What is viral meningitis?" he asked.

"It's a swelling of the cover of the brain and the doctors don't even know if she will live!" I was sobbing hysterically.

He stood up, walked to the kitchen, threw his empty beer bottle in the trash, turned back toward me. "I'm sorry" he said, and I could see the sheen of tears in his eyes, "but I can't handle this. " He walked out the door and I heard his car roaring down the driveway. I couldn't believe his attitude! Our baby was seriously ill and he couldn't handle it? I was asleep before he returned and that was all that was said.

The next 20 days were spent in a kind of sleepwalking pattern. Roy got up early in the morning and went to work. I got up after he was gone, killed a bit of time with household chores, and then went to the hospital to sit in the waiting room until they let me in to see my baby. In the evenings at home, the television was on and neither of us had the energy or will to get beyond the impasse.

There was no change in Samantha. She was always asleep when I saw her. The nurses told me that they were doing spinal taps twice a week, which was apparently the only way they could measure her progress, or lack thereof. Finally, in the middle of the third week, one of the nurses said, "Would you like to hold her? She is no longer contagious. Her sixth spinal tap was clear and she will be able to go home soon." One nurse carefully picked her up and placed her in my arms while another nurse held onto the IV tubes that were still attached to her. It felt blissful to be able to touch her and I vowed that when I got her home I would cuddle her, make her understand how much I loved her, and help her forget all this torture she had endured. I took her home two days later, confident that the ordeal was over, that she was well and everything would be all right.

CHAPTER THREE

Home from the hospital

She slept a great deal her first days at home. When she was awake, she just lay quietly in her crib looking around, but she did not cry. When I held her, she didn't cuddle into my arms, just remained passive. When she was finished with her bottle, she had projectile vomiting and lost most of what she had taken in. In the evening after her bath and pajama time, Roy and I put her between us in our big bed. When Sam came home from the hospital, Roy became a tender, caring father. We talked to her, sang to her, kissed her, did all the loving things parents of new babies do. She never responded, just lay there looking at us with big, round, wide-open eyes. She had given me enough signals that she wanted to be left alone, so one evening I propped her bottle so she could drink it in her crib. She drank it down eagerly, then turned her head to the side and gave a little smile. It was the first smile I had seen and there was no projectile vomiting!

When I took her to Dr. Hollis for her two-month checkup, I described those things: her lack of response to us, her vomiting that stopped when I let her have her bottle in bed, her silence. He said, "You have to give her time to get over the trauma she's been through. Be patient! She will be alright."

I kept on worrying about her because I wasn't hearing any "cooing" or "babbling" that are normal baby sounds. In addition to that, she had developed a new technique of avoiding eye contact. Whenever we would bend over to talk to her, she would jam her right hand into her mouth and hold her left hand over her eyes. When we picked her up, she would turn her body so that her back was pressed against us. Each month that passed brought some new odd behavior that was convincing me that something was wrong.

She learned to sit up when she was six months old and then she refused to lie down. She slept sitting up in a corner of her crib. When she learned how to crawl, she couldn't figure out how to maneuver around objects. If she bumped into chair legs or tables, she would just keep butting her head or shoulders against it until I rescued her. When it was time to start introducing soft foods into her diet, it was way too intimidating for her to have me sit in front of her and try to put a small spoon in her mouth. Time after time she would clamp her mouth shut and whip her head to one side, which, of course, sent the baby food flying. I finally gave up and prepared things she could pick up like small pieces of bread softened with broth, or mashed potatoes.

She learned to walk at about one year old and along with that came another new behavior. My too-silent, passive little girl began having screaming tantrums. It was very puzzling because they just came out of the blue for no apparent reason. My response was to pick her up, wrap her in a blanket, and sit down in a rocking chair. Holding her tight with her back to me, I would rock vigorously while singing "My Darling Clementine". It worked and she would be calm and quiet before I finished all the verses of the song.

Throughout all of this, I took her for monthly checkups with the pediatrician, Dr. Hollis. He would say things like, "Well, maybe her development is lagging a little, but just give her time and she'll catch up".

After Roy realized that Samantha was not "normal", he was not sure that it was a good idea to have a second baby. In my first marriage my two daughters were born thirteen months apart and I remembered how much fun it was to see how close they were, how much they enjoyed each other's company, how much they loved each other. I wanted that kind of companionship for Samantha as opposed to being brought up as an only child. He finally agreed and when Samantha was 4 months old, I was pregnant with my fifth child and was certain it would be a girl.

Roy was still employed by the shop that made automobile parts and he had an excellent Blue Shield insurance plan that had fully covered the enormous cost of Samantha's three-week stay in the hospital. However, about the time that I got pregnant with our second baby, he had been laid off and, although he was working in a friend's service station, he had no insurance coverage. After our experience with Sam's hospitalization, I felt it was imperative to have insurance coverage for the new baby. I had worked as a secretary for 15 years when my first three children were growing up and I had an excellent résumé. So I went to work in the office of American Seating Company in Grand Rapids. My company insurance would be effective 60 days after my employment.

My sister, Nina, had been running a licensed child-care business in her home for the past five years and she welcomed my four month old Samantha into her little group of children. She had read many books on the subject of child development and shared my concern about the lack of normal milestones in Samantha's life. She found Sam's remoteness very troubling. She said, "When I put her in her little sling chair, she shows no interest in the other children who are playing around her. But when I put her in her crib, she is perfectly content to lie there and watch the breeze ruffle the curtains. I recently came across an article about "autism". Have you ever heard of it?"

I had to admit that I had not, but I would check it out. I started with the dictionary first. Definition: Autism (n): a disturbance in psychological development in which use of language, reaction to stimuli, interpretation of the world, and the formation of relationships are not fully established and follow unusual patterns.

Wow! This is a description of Samantha!

I took Samantha to Dr. Hollis intending to discuss autism with him during her one-year checkup. He gave me the usual: "She is doing just fine. Her height and weight are in the normal range for her age. She looks as healthy as can be."

During all of her past checkups, she had been sitting on an examination table and I had been holding onto her. I was seething with anger with his comments, so I decided he really needed to see her in action. I put her down on her feet and let go of her. She started her performance with a couple of spins (a recent addition to her behavior repertoire), then ran back and forth around his office, touching everything she could reach, pulling things down onto the floor.

The doctor looked as if he couldn't believe what he was seeing. He said "Here now!" and reached out to grab her. The result of that move was a full-fledged screaming tantrum.

I was standing there with my arms folded, thinking, "Go, Sam! Show him!"

His face had turned beet red and his eyes had widened behind his glasses as he stared at my out of control child.

I picked her up. She stopped screaming and squirmed around to her usual position with her back to me. I said, "I think she is autistic."

He sighed and then said: "Take her home and love her, but don't expect anything from her."

This man had been my pediatrician for all three of my older children. Needless to say, that was the end of our 20-year relationship.

CHAPTER FOUR

Searching for Help

Our next pediatrician was Dr. Patricia Cotton. She was at least 20 years younger than Dr. Hollis and she also knew what autism is. She agreed that many of the things I had observed in Samantha's development were consistent with what she had read about autistic children. She also said that we needed to get therapy for her at a very early age. She telephoned me a few days after our first consultation. She had a no-nonsense attitude and a wonderful melodious voice.

"I've been doing some searching and I think I have found a school that might be right for Samantha" she said enthusiastically. "You need to go check it out and then you will need to contact the school board in your area because it will be their responsibility to provide transportation and tuition".

The next day, Samantha and I made the trip to the North end of Grand Rapids to observe Lincoln School. It was established for children with moderate to severe cognitive impairment. The teacher that Samantha would be dealing with was small, blond, and very pretty. She introduced herself as "Carolyn". She had a half dozen children who appeared to be about the same age as Sammie. Several were in wheelchairs; some were lying on cushions on the floor, and some were strapped into small chairs. She asked me to sit on the floor and hold Samantha in my lap. She sat across from us and the first thing she did was lean close to Samantha and say, in a gentle voice, "Sammie, look at me." Sammie did her usual avoidance thing. One hand jammed against her mouth between her thumb and forefinger and the other hand in front of her eyes. The next thing Carolyn did was hold out a small box of raisins. She shook the box to get Samantha's attention, then opened it up to show her the raisins. Then closed the box and handed it to her. Samantha dropped the box on the floor and paid no more attention to it. Carolyn said, "The normal reaction for a child of this age (12 months) would be curiosity. She should be trying to open the box."

She observed Samantha for a few more minutes and then said, "This child is autistic and there is a school over on the South side of town that would be a better fit for her." She went into her office, called the director of the other school and made an appointment for us. Following her directions, I drove about 20 miles South to the very edge of Grand Rapids. There was a sign in front of a small, new-looking building that said: Kent County Special Education. We entered into a long hallway that had windows on one side that overlooked a fenced play yard. The other side had what we would learn were called "cubbies". Wooden cubbyholes had been built against the wall. Each was perhaps 2 feet wide and 4 feet tall and there were about 30 of them. The wall above contained windows into the classrooms. Each cubbie was labeled with a child's name written in crayon on bright-colored paper. There was a wooden coat hook in each that held jackets, scarves, and backpacks. Across the bottom was a row of built-in benches. All of my first impressions were good ones. It looked clean, tidy, bright colors and well organized. It looked like they recognized each child as an individual.

We found the office marked "Administration" and an older woman came around the desk and introduced herself as Mrs. Jackson. She asked Samantha's name and age and then said," Miss Rollins will take Samantha to Classroom 1 while you and I talk". A young woman appeared in the office door, gently took Sam's hand and walked out. I was very nervous and beginning to think that it was a very bad idea to put my baby in this place. She was too little, too young to go to school.

Mrs. Jackson had returned to her desk, opened a drawer and drew out a folder that turned out to be forms I would need to fill out. Application forms for her school, for the Lowell School District, one to be signed by the pediatrician, Dr. Cotton. All that was needed from me was my name and address, Samantha's name and age, and one for my permission to send all those forms out to the people who would decide whether Samantha could be enrolled in this school. When we were finished, she closed the folder, stood up and said, "OK. Let's go see how Samantha is doing."

We went to Classroom 1 where Samantha was just sitting on the floor looking toward the window. There were five or six children of varying sizes and ages sitting at small tables and several aides helping them with activities. Some were coloring on large sheets of paper, some were trying to put together puzzles that had a few large wooden pieces, and there was one larger boy who was throwing a temper tantrum. He was seated in a chair with straps buckled around his chest, the teacher was holding the chair so it wouldn't fall over and the boy was howling and trying to throw himself around. The anguished expression on the boy's face as he tried to free himself from the straps was more than I could bear! I picked Samantha up and got out of there as fast as I could. I was in the last month of pregnancy and decided to postpone my search for therapy for Samantha until the new baby was born and Sammie was a little older.

Andrea Kay Brown was born on the 10th of June, 1972. She weighed 10 pounds 6 ounces and she was beautiful. She had dark hair and would later have brown eyes. She was born one day before my insurance at American Seating would be effective. Fortunately, there were no problems and Roy went back to work in the job shop a few days later and his insurance was reinstated. I telephoned American Seating and told them I was not coming back to work. I felt very guilty for not giving them the usual three weeks notice and I never added them to my resume.

My oldest daughter, Karen, had turned 18, graduated from Lowell High School and bought her first car with her earnings from Jimmy's Grill. She and her best friend, Kathy, found a small low-rent apartment in Grand Rapids and set out on their own.

My second daughter, Laura, was 17 and she had become a very accomplished equestrienne. She had a trunk full of ribbons and trophies. Her trainer had bought a stable about 40 miles from us. He thought she had enough skill to compete in larger, more professional horse shows. He and his wife offered her room and board in their home where he would continue to train her. After much pleading on her part and a promise that she would finish school, I reluctantly let her go. It was a dream come true for her.

That left only 15 year old Larry home on the farm. He was a shy, thin, sensitive boy. It wasn't long before he and Roy started running into trouble. Larry wanted to do the farm chores the way we had always done them; Roy wanted to do things his way. One day they were working together trying to repair the John Deere tractor. It was a weekend, a hot one, and Roy had been drinking beer most of the day. Larry reached out to straighten a drive belt just as Roy was about to start the engine. Larry could have lost his hand. Roy lost his temper and yelled a few choice epithets at the top of his voice. Larry yelled back, trying to defend his action. I stepped out the door just in time to see Roy punch Larry in the face hard enough to knock him down. Roy yelled, "Just get the hell out of my way!" Larry came in the house with blood pouring out of a cut on his cheekbone. There were tears in his eyes, but he was trying not to cry. He said, in a voice choked with the unshed tears," Mom, I hate him! I can't live here anymore!"

I patched up his face and then called his father and asked if Larry could come stay with him for a while. Larry packed some clothing and then sat in his room until his father got there. I watched him go down the driveway and get in the car. He never looked back. Then Roy got in his car and went speeding toward the town of Lowell, presumably to do some more drinking. I was left there alone with two little babies and I felt like my heart was breaking. Roy returned the following morning, all contrite, apologetic, and hung over. I didn't even bother to ask him where he had been.

Samantha was now a year and a half old and there was no change in her development. She was still not developing any speech, still wasn't interacting with Roy or me. She was curious about her sister Andrea, though, and when the baby cried, Sammie would press her ear against her face and listen with a puzzled look on her face. I had also discovered that she was impervious to pain. I had seen her bump head first into a car bumper hard enough to knock her down. She didn't cry, she just got up and continued on her way.

That big, old, 5-bedroom farmhouse felt awfully empty with just Roy, me, and the babies. We weren't even using the upstairs rooms. There was a large dining room that now contained two cribs. The house was heated with fuel oil. When I bought the place, fuel oil cost 14 cents a gallon. The price had been creeping up and was now a whopping one dollar a gallon. Also, my savings account with the Shell Oil "retirement" money was running low. As much as I loved that old farmhouse and the outbuildings, it was about to bleed the bank account dry. The obvious solution was to sell the place. I came up with the idea of selling the house and 15 acres. We could keep 5 acres and build a small house. There was a nice open space between the old place and the next house. There was a flat space that dipped down toward the road. . I drew up a floor plan for a 2 bedroom house that could be built with a walk-out basement. We took the rough sketch to a builder, he drew up an architectural plan and told us he could build it for $18,000. We put the old place on the market for $30,000 and it sold within 2 months, with a contingency that we could live there until our new house was finished. Everything went according to plan and before long, we moved into our new house.

CHAPTER FIVE

Sammie's first school

It was 1974 and Samantha was 3 years old. It was time for me to fill out those applications, contact the Lowell School Board, and get her enrolled in school. It took several months to get this accomplished and then one day one of those little yellow school buses pulled into our yard to transport her the 20 miles to Kent County Special Education. When the driver opened the door, however, the first thing I saw was a small boy (probably about 2 years old) hanging off one of the seats! He had a seat belt around his waist, but had managed to slip half out of it and stand on the floor. There were no shoulder restraints. I asked the driver to wait for me, ran back to the house and hastily grabbed the diaper bag, a couple of bottles, and Andrea. All three of us went to school that day! When we got back home that afternoon, I got out my sewing machine and made a vest that, when combined with the seatbelt, would hold Samantha in her seat. All in all, her first day in the classroom went well and I was very glad to have been there to observe.

At the end of her first week in school I received this report from her teacher: "Sammie had a good week. We have been able to get more contact out of her than I had expected which pleased me. She has had two shows of temper and cried. I'm not sure what brought them on. However, she came out of them fairly well. I took her on a trampoline earlier this week. She enjoyed it so much that I think it will be a good place to work with her."

Samantha's second week of school was apparently easier for her. She was much more calm, less hyperactive. In fact, the only outer sign of stress was her hand biting. Over the weekend she was more sociable than usual with us with less time spent alone in her room and more time spent trying to play with Andrea. She had brought a finger painting home from school and I taped it on the kitchen wall. She spent at least 5 minutes quietly sitting on a chair and looking at her painting!

Over the next few months, the school continued to report improvements in Sammie's development. She learned to drink out of a cup by herself after some initial help. After a week of practice, she could take some plastic circles and put them on a peg. A recent improvement at home was that she was cooperating when I dressed her. She would lift her feet to step into pants and try to get her arms into sleeves. This was a very welcome and highly praised improvement.

Roy and I had been getting along well and he was working steadily in the job shop. He normally got out of work at 3 o'clock and was home at 3:30, but suddenly he started going to a tavern with his co-workers. They would drink beer and play poker. It started out innocently enough, but it escalated until he was losing serious money. Apparently when he was losing, he wouldn't quit playing so there were times that he didn't come home at all and didn't have any money in his pocket when he did come back. I told him that since he wasn't bringing home a paycheck, I would have to get a job. There was a factory in Lowell advertising for workers for their 4 to midnight shift, so if he would get home by 3:30, I would be able to get there in time. My thinking was that if he had to be home to take care of Samantha and Andrea, he wouldn't be able to continue playing after work.

The factory was equipped with huge extrusion machines that hissed and clanked and spit out plastic forms for chairs. These would be sent to American Seating to be upholstered. How ironic! I had worked as a secretary in their sales office and now I was going to work a night shift on an assembly line providing raw materials for them! The foreman put me to work as soon as the interview was over. I had to catch the forms, drill 4 holes in the seat and then trim them with a knife to assure a smooth outer edge before the machine belched out the next one. It was hot, smelly hard work and my first night on the job, I lost 5 pounds! I got home at 12:30 and slept until 5 am. Then it was my turn to take care of the little girls.

I worked there for about 3 weeks and then one night when I got home, the house was empty. There was a smashed beer bottle that had been thrown against the wall in the kitchen. I telephoned Roy's sister Shannon to see if she knew where he had taken my little girls. She said, "The girls are safe here with me. Roy was drunk and has gone to see his ex-wife! Your little ones are fine. They are both asleep."

I asked her to keep them and I would drive up to get them in the morning. I was frantic! The thought of him in a drunken rage driving 40 miles with Samantha and Andrea in the car made me physically ill! The thought of him being with his ex-wife made me furious! I knew our marriage was over. I had had all I was going to take. I sat down and thought about all that had gone on in the five years Roy and I had been together. He had shown some alcoholic tendencies early on, but he was getting worse. I thought if I did something really drastic, maybe I could shock him into realizing what he was doing to himself and our relationship. I wrote him the following letter:

> "Roy: Since you have decided to go back to your ex-wife, I have decided to leave. You can move her into this house along with her two kids and our two babies. I will deed the house to you if you will promise to take good care of Sam and Andy. Goodbye and good luck. Sue"

I called Shannon to tell her what I was going to do and asked her to keep Samantha and Andrea until Roy contacted her. Then I went to the airport in Grand Rapids and bought a ticket on a flight to Los Angeles. Tears rolled down my face throughout the flight. My sister lived in Anaheim so I called her and she came to LAX to pick me up. I called my mom so she would know where I was and what was going on.

The second day later Roy started burning up the telephone wires begging me to come back home. The same old story: he was so sorry, he would never do it again, he would stop drinking, could I please just forgive him. If I had brought Samantha and Andrea with me, I would never have gone back, but I was dying without my babies!

I had read an article in my sister's LA newspaper about advances that were being made in special education in California. In addition to schools, the article said that employers were arranging on-site child care. That sounded like the solution to my problems. I told Roy that I thought the only way we could salvage our marriage would be to make a new start in a whole new place. I knew by then that he would never be able to keep his promises, but I needed his help to get to California.

CHAPTER SIX

California here we come

We sold the house and everything in it and bought a small motor home. We left Michigan with just our clothing, a television set, 50 quart jars of tomatoes and peaches that I had canned in the summer, and one box with just enough dishes and cooking utensils to use on the trip. We had taken a weekend trial run earlier to see if Samantha would be able to tolerate the trip. She had been just fine, so we thought she would be okay. We were wrong. About the third day on the road I guess she thought she was going to have to live in that motor home forever. She became very agitated, threw screaming tantrums when we tried to fasten her in her seat, refused to let me hold her. When none of that ended the trip, she started biting and scratching herself until her arms and her face were bleeding. I had to put my white socks on her hands and fasten them with masking tape. She still tried to bite herself, but wasn't able to do so much damage.

We arrived at my sister's house in Anaheim on Christmas Eve 1975. Roy and I agreed almost immediately that LA was not for us! The following day we set out in the motor home again. Our plan was to drive North on Highway 101 until we saw a town we thought might fit our needs. We said we would follow the coast all the way to Seattle, Washington, if necessary. When we got to Santa Barbara it was such a pretty town we decided that we should check it out. The first priority was to find out if there was a school for Samantha. What we found was Hollister School located, not in Santa Barbara, but in the small town that bordered it, Goleta. My directory said the school was established to teach autistic children. We had just found our new home and what a beautiful place it was! Goleta is bordered on the North by mountains and on the South by the Pacific Ocean.

The local newspaper advertised several affordable houses for rent and we found the perfect one. It was vacant and we were able to move right in. Samantha and Andrea ran back and forth through all the empty rooms, then out the patio door to the fenced back yard. They giggled and shrieked and had a wonderful time. I am sure it was like being let out of jail after being cooped up in the motor home for that long trip!

Roy found a furniture store and bought a queen size bed for us and two twin beds for the girls. The next day he went looking for a car for me. He found a 1948 Ford that was in good condition and ran very nicely. In Michigan, a 30 year old car would have been rusted through from all the salt on the roads in winter. We were very impressed with the car's nice body.

The following day I loaded Samantha and Andrea in the "new" car and went to the local Social Service office to find out how to get Samantha registered in school. They sent us to Tri-Counties Regional Center where we met Kathy Hunter who would become Sammie's caseworker and our very good friend for the next 14 years. Kathy made arrangements for Samantha to be enrolled in Hollister School. We were directed to a small four-room building located behind a large elementary school. I would soon learn that there was a State directive that required special education students to be "mainstreamed" with the regular elementary students. This separate building on the campus was Santa Barbara County's response to mainstreaming.

We introduced ourselves to the teacher. She took Sammie by the hand and settled her into a chair at a child-size table with 4 children who appeared to be about the same age as she was. An aide was monitoring them and I was impressed with the calm, orderly atmosphere. The teacher's name was Hannah and she asked me to sit down and tell her about Samantha's level of development.

About 3 weeks later, I received a letter from the Santa Barbara County school superintendent's office regarding the educational planning and placement of Samantha. The needs that were established for Sammy were: 1.) that she needs to increase contact with adults (eye and body contact and to follow simple directions; 2.) to eliminate inappropriate behavior, i.e., scratching, biting, hyperventilation, and withdrawing; 3.)

needs behavior management for tantrums and aggression toward adults and peers; 4.) needs remediation of cognitive skills.

The educational objectives written to meet these needs include the following statements: 1.) when given 10 pegs, Sammy will put them into a pegboard independently; 2.) when given rings and pegs, Sammy will sort them into their appropriate piles with 100% accuracy; 3.) when given directions "come here", "sit down", "look at me", Sammy will respond with 95% accuracy; 4.) when given a clothespin, Sammy will be able to independently pinch and put it on the edge of a box or can; 5.) when placed on a large handle ball, Sammy will relax and remain relaxed on the ball without resistance for 20 minutes; 6.) when in a group setting, Sammy will sit in a chair for 20 minutes without prompting, and 7.) when presented with an obstacle course of a table, tunnel, and yellow line, Sammy will be able to track what she is to do and remain on task for the duration of the course.

The final recommendation was that Sammy would remain in the Hollister School Autism Project.

From the time we left Michigan, Roy had been on his best behavior. He spent his days searching for a permanent job, working part-time for a local landscaper, and scouring yard sales to replace things we had left behind. He discovered that "moving sales" held after a home sale were great bargains. Our house was soon well furnished with a sofa, end tables, lamps, dressers and a king-size bed. At the same time, money was running very low. It was time for me to get another job.

I found a job in Montecito, a city South of Santa Barbara that is inhabited for the most part by millionaires. My new boss is one of them. My job is to do the secretarial work for his bookkeeper. He comes into the office (whenever he is in the mood to do so), dictates a letter or two (which I take down in shorthand). The rest of my job is to update a filing system that keeps track of his race horses. The old nursery rhyme keeps running through my mind: "The king is in his counting house, counting out his money". I do not like this man! And, besides that, when I leave the office in the evening, the sun is blinding me as I drive back North toward Goleta. I began actively looking for a different job right after I started this one.

I enrolled 4 year old Andrea in a pre-school called Kids-N-Things.

She cried the first few mornings when I dropped her off, but soon began to run ahead of me, eager to see her new friends.

I found a very nice 16 year old girl in our neighborhood who could work as Samantha's babysitter when she returned from school in the afternoons. Roy took care of her in the mornings after I left for work and then he was free of family duty until dinner time in the evening.

This arrangement worked out well for approximately two months and then one Friday night Roy did not return home. He was gone all weekend. When he showed up again on Sunday evening, he was broke and badly hung over. I had spent the weekend feeling betrayed; extremely angry; frightened at the prospect of starting over again on my own and, this time, with 2 young girls to parent by myself. He knew me well enough by now to realize that I would not tolerate his alcoholism. When I told him that the marriage was over, that I was going to start divorce proceedings in the morning, he apologized for his failure to live up to his part of our bargain, packed up his belongings and left the house.

For the next few days, he apparently just drank and enjoyed his freedom. He telephoned a couple of times to see if I had had a change of heart, but otherwise left us alone. When I asked him where my attorney could get in touch with him, he said, "He can find me at Gus's Bar!"

After that he finally realized that I was serious and that he could not come back. He began making threatening phone calls. I could tell that he was drunk and didn't pay a lot of attention to his rambling threats until he said that he was carrying a machete and was "coming after me". I called the police and they came to the house to talk to me. They said they couldn't do anything without a restraining order. They did, however, go to Gus's bar and talk to Roy, but they did not find a machete. Two evenings after that, Roy came to my door. Andrea let him in, saying: "Hi, Daddy", with a big smile, glad to see her daddy again. He ignored her, stalked out to the kitchen where I was preparing dinner. He thundered in a big, angry voice: "WHAT'S THE IDEA OF CALLING THE COPS ON ME!" He grabbed me and slapped me. He was in a terrible, drunken rage and I knew I only had one chance of avoiding serious injury. I let my body go limp and I refused to look at him. It was exactly the right thing to do because he made a disgusted sound and threw me into the dining room table hard enough that it collapsed. He turned and stalked back out of the house. I called the police again and they came back to the house, but they told me there wasn't anything they could do. After they left, I locked all the doors and windows and set about "booby-trapping" the house just in case he returned. In the kitchen I put an open can of pepper by the door and a cast iron skillet on the counter by the window. In the living room, I put the fireplace poker next to the patio doors. In the bedroom, I placed a hard wood baseball bat on my bed. Fortunately for him, he never showed up again. When the divorce was complete, the court mailed his papers to him at Gus's Bar!

My 4 year old Andrea witnessed all of this and listened to the police when they came to talk to me. Since that time, she has never once acknowledged Roy as her father.

PART TWO

CHAPTER SEVEN

Hollister School Autism Class

Samantha, in the meantime, was making great progress in Hollister School's Autism Class. Her receptive language and matching programs were especially good. In order to keep her program consistent, the teachers and I started sending a journal back and forth with her. I wrote in it in the morning describing how things were going at home and they wrote in it in the afternoon before they sent her back. This procedure followed her all the way through her school life.

<u>Notes from Samantha's Journal: February 19, 1976</u>
Teacher: Samantha did a great job (independently) of tearing up lettuce for a salad. She wouldn't eat much as I made her use a spoon.

Sue (Mother): Sammie's screech-rate is way down and sitting time is way up. She's been awake since about 3 am so don't be surprised if she tires early today.

She has a speech therapist for an hour a day at school and I was taught by the therapist (whose name happened to be Sammy) how to practice her techniques at home. As a result, Samantha has two word-sounds: "Ta" for Stop and "E" for Eat. Every evening after dinner she and I sat at the table with a tape recorder and a carton of yogurt. The therapist advised me to start with vowel sounds "a" "e" "i" "o" "u" and at first to reinforce any sound with praise and a small bit of yogurt. The tape recorder was used to assess her progress.

Samantha also has a new friend at school. Her name is Via and their interaction started on the playground. At first Via began pulling

Sam around and then they began playing a kind of tag. Sam runs off, looking over her shoulder, and Via chases her and catches her. They walk around together for a few minutes and then Sammie runs off and starts the game over.

Samantha was still in diapers when she started school and toilet training became a priority with the teacher and aides. They started by putting her on the potty every half hour to get a baseline on exactly when (if possible) she goes. They requested a supply of training pants because it was hard to pull Pampers up and down all day. They reported a few successes between the failures. I got a potty chair for her at home and followed their example. After a few days I wrote the following note in her journal: "This morning Samantha sat on the potty when she had to go! If she had pulled down her pants, it would have been perfect. At least it means she's getting the right idea."

Samantha's Journal: February 24
Sue: Sammie had a very bad evening from 6 pm on. She screamed, cried, scratched and threw herself around. The worst time she has had since we've been here. I finally took her for a walk (in the rain) and after that she was OK. I've put lotion on all the new scratches this morning and hope she leaves them alone today. When I got her dressed this morning, she said "Ba, ba, ba" and headed for the door. It is the first time in months that she has tried to use the few words she has.

Teacher: She started out really wild this morning, but got better after a couple of sessions.

Good news: Santa Barbara Research Center called me in for an interview and I will start working for them as an Administrative Secretary. They are located in Goleta about 5 minutes drive from our house. This will make my schedule much, much easier. Kids-N-Things (Andrea's day-care) is just a few blocks from SBRC and Hollister School is less than 5 miles away.

Today, April 21st, 1977, is Samantha's sixth birthday. I always get a little sad on her birthdays. Birthdays are milestones and Sam's development is lagging. She should be starting kindergarten but instead she is trying to develop speech, using a little bit of sign language, and learning to use the potty chair. I know we are making progress and I am grateful for all the work that is being done in her classroom, but birthdays still just seem to jump up and bite me!

I could no longer afford the rent on the house, so the three of us are moving again. There is a moderately-priced building on the same street as Kids-N-Things and I rented a second floor apartment. Our babysitter, Joan, rounded up some neighborhood boys to help carry furniture up the stairs. She had her driver's license now and is more valuable to us than ever. I really don't know how I would have ever managed without all of her help.

Now school is out for the summer and Joan comes to the apartment every weekday to care for both Samantha and Andrea. The new neighborhood is within walking distance of the beach and all three girls love spending time there. There is also a small park nearby with swings, slides, and climbing equipment. Both Joan and Andrea practice speech and signs with Samantha so she doesn't forget before she goes back to school. My new workplace (SBRC) is less than 5 minutes away, so I am able to go home at noon to fix lunch for the 4 of us.

Sammie is pairing speech sounds with signing. She says "ee" and puts her open palm on her face or chin when she wants to eat. She says "mm" for more and "ta" for stop. She can also say "Mama". Tears rolled down my face the first time I heard that! I have waited 5 years to hear her say Mama. Her receptive language now includes "come here" "sit down" "go to the door" "close the door".

On June 10th, 1977, Andrea was five years old. She is amazing! She is pretty, smart, loving. There aren't enough adjectives to describe her. She has been through an awful lot for such a little girl. She seems to come through all of our crises with equilibrium. She loves her sister in spite of having her sleep interrupted by Samantha's night wakefulness and sometimes being on the receiving end of Sam's violence. When Samantha throws a tantrum, she throws herself around and hits anyone within her range.

Andrea has a very sunny nature and I have never seen her throw a tantrum. I think of her as my little shiny star and I love her dearly.

CHAPTER EIGHT

Alan

My personal life has improved lately. SBRC has a coffee area in a hallway near my office. The company provides free coffee and it is dispensed from a 30 cup coffeemaker. Most of the secretaries fill thermoses for their bosses shortly after we get to work. While waiting my turn to get my boss's coffee, I have noticed a very nice looking man standing there patiently waiting to fill his cup. He has been there several days at the same time I am. He is not wearing a wedding ring, so I asked one of the secretaries about him. Secretaries know everything that goes on in the company, so I knew I would be given a run-down on his status. They told me that his name was Alan, that he was an electrical engineer, and also that he was recently divorced. The next time I saw him at the coffee machine, I smiled at him and asked if he would like to go ahead of me in line to fill his cup before I filled my thermos. He smiled back and said, "No, thanks. Your boss needs his morning coffee. I can wait." He had a great smile and beautiful blue eyes. I knew that I wanted to get acquainted with him!

Later that day, we ran into each other again at the Xerox machine. There was no one else around so we chatted for a few minutes. The annual Mexican Fiesta was just starting in downtown Santa Barbara, so I said, "Will you be going to the fiesta?" I thought that was a good opening and that if he was interested in getting acquainted with me, he might ask me to accompany him. No such luck! He said, "No, I'm not going to it this year". I was disappointed and turned to go back to my office. "Sue," he called, "would you like to have lunch with me?"

Oh, Good! He wasn't blowing me off! He was interested in getting acquainted with me! We made arrangements to have lunch the next day at his house. He said he would cook burgers and French fries. Wow! A man who offered to cook! This was getting better by the minute!

He picked me up at noon for the five minute drive to his house. He lived only a few blocks from the apartment I was renting. When we walked into his house, I was shocked. My first impression was that the livingroom was dark. There was bright red carpeting on the floor, blue draperies that were closed over patio doors, and, oh my gosh, horrible-looking big knives hanging on the walls! My first thought was, "What have I gotten myself into this time?" I was frightened and trying to think of a way to get out of there! He said, "Come sit down in the dining room and I will start lunch." He sounded harmless enough, so I followed him and sat down at the table. He prepared a frosty-looking rum and coke (light on the rum for me). While he was cooking, he told me that his wife had left him "to go find herself" and had left her two boys behind. One was 13 (Mark) and one was 8 years old (Frank). I told him that I had two little girls, one of whom was handicapped. The more we talked about ourselves, the more I relaxed. He told me that he belonged to a historical arms club and that the knives on the wall were awards he had won at club shows. I was convinced that this was a good man; a little quirky maybe, but not dangerous.

A few days later, I invited him to my apartment to meet my daughters. I served him coffee and cookies. He had prepared dinner for his boys and helped with homework, so it was late evening when he arrived and Andrea and Samantha were already in bed. We were sitting on the sofa when Sammie came out of the bedroom and climbed up between us. She stared at him for a few minutes with a solemn expression on her face, then walked behind him as he scooted forward and gave her room to do so. She sat down on the arm of the sofa and stared at him for a few more minutes, then hopped down and went back to bed. Neither of us had said a word as she made her inspection. If Alan had spoken, or tried to touch her, she probably would have turned and run back to her room. . It was just a kind of enchanted moment.

From that time on, Alan and I continued to see each other whenever we could. Our weekend activities revolved around all four kids. We spent a lot of time at the beach because that was a favorite thing for all of them. Alan's favorite thing was the Saturday morning swap meet where he searched for things he might add to his militaria collection. I had taken over cooking dinner (which Alan surrendered eagerly) and we ate together as a family.

Alan and Mark were both very tender and solicitous with Samantha. When Alan discovered that she would not allow herself to be held facing another person, he decided to see if he could do something about it. He showed her a cookie and then put it up on the fireplace mantel. Then he held out his arms and said, "Do you want the cookie?" Of course she wanted the cookie, so she let him pick her up so she could reach it. After they played that game a few times, she was so interested in getting the cookie that she forgot to squirm away from him. She allowed herself to be picked up in a normal face to face way for the first time in her life. Mark watched his dad and decided to see if he could get her to do the same for him and she did. That did not mean, however, that she no longer squirmed away from others. Many more people suffered bruised breastbones when they set her on their lap and she squirmed around and banged her head into them!

CHAPTER NINE

Garfield School for Trainable Mentally Retarded

September 1977. I have just been informed by the Director of Special Education that Hollister Autism School has been closed down. Samantha has been reassigned to Garfield School's Trainable Mentally Retarded class. I have met with her new teacher, Vivian Olson. Neither she nor I can understand why Samantha has been assigned to her classroom. In the first place, she doesn't know anything about autism and, in the second place, she has 5 students and NO AIDES!

I called Kathy H., Sam's caseworker, at Tri Counties Regional Center and complained about this new placement. To begin with, I told her that Samantha didn't belong in a TMR class. There is very little connection between mental retardation and autism. Secondly, Mrs. Olson has had no training or experience in dealing with a child like Samantha. Kathy talked with the Special Education Director and reported back to me that there was no other suitable placement available. I never did find out what they did with all of the other Hollister students! I finally agreed to accept the Garfield School placement, but only if Samantha had a one-to-one aide.

Another problem with this new placement is transportation. This school is located close to Santa Barbara and Samantha will have to ride on the little yellow school bus. The bus gets to our neighborhood after 8:30 am and I have to be at work by 8. I had become well acquainted with Marnie Jones, the owner of Kids N' Things Nursery School. Although Andrea no longer needed her service because she was in kindergarten, I made arrangements with Marnie to allow Samantha to sit in her office for that half hour until the bus picked her up. Samantha also needed after school care from about 4 pm until I got there a little after 5 pm. Kathy H. (caseworker, Tri-Counties Regional Center) made arrangements to fund and provide an aide for that period of time. Since Samantha cannot communicate, I have never left her without knowing the person or having some kind of supervision. Again Marnie agreed to have Samantha dropped off at Kids N' Things along with the aide that Kathy would provide. This arrangement worked out very well and before long Marnie was included as another part of Samantha's team.

When Samantha started riding on the bus again, I had to make her another vest that would keep her secure in her seat. The busses still only have lap belts, no shoulder straps, and Samantha can wiggle out of her seat.

Within the first week, I received a phone call from Mrs. Olson saying that she was overwhelmed with Sam's behavior. She said she was having to spend 75% of her class time dealing with Samantha and that it was not fair to her other students. I knew she was right because I had observed her class. Her sweet, little TMR kids were calm and quiet and Samantha was like a whirlwind in comparison. I told her that I had been promised a one-to-one aide and thought one would soon be assigned.

A month later Kathy H. told me she had been told that no aide would be provided because there just wasn't money available to do so. This prompted me to write the following letter to the Director of Special Education:

"This letter is being written out of concern for the education of my autistic child, Samantha Jo Brown, who is presently enrolled in the Garfield School class for Trainable Mentally Retarded. One of the contingencies for Sammie's acceptance in that classroom was that there would be an aide provided to help keep her disruptive behaviors under control. At every conference and consultation, Mrs. Olson has repeatedly stated that Sammie needs one-to-one attention at least 75% of the time to keep her on task. We all assumed that an aide was going to be provided, but now we are being told it is impossible because someone failed to allow for it in the budget.

At our most recent conference Mrs. Olson said that it is unfair and unrealistic to expect her to deal with Samantha 75% of the time and that, therefore, if an aide is not provided, Sam will find herself "set aside" and just not taught.

In dealing with the Santa Barbara school system in general, and Garfield School in particular, I have found people to be sympathetic to Sam's needs and cooperative beyond what should be expected of them. Sam has progressed, matured and definitely benefited from their help. When I hear Mrs. Olson's negative comments, I have to believe that she has been pushed to her limit.

In order to keep Samantha in that classroom and in order to maintain the progress she is presently making, I am hereby requesting once again that an aide be placed in her classroom as soon as possible. I would hope it could be accomplished before the first of the year."

Finally, in desperation, Mrs. Olson put Samantha on roller skates! She reported to me: "This requires her full attention and consequently she makes no noises or strange hand motions. This week she has sat through a 15 minute movie and 20 minutes of music with very few noises!"

When I got that note, I went ballistic and fired off another letter to the Director:

"I have been very disappointed not to receive any acknowledgement of my letter requesting a one-to-one aide for Samantha. Please see the attached copy of a note I received from Mrs. Olson. Roller skates? Is this a method of teaching, or the beginning of Samantha being set aside as threatened? She is already handicapped and definitely does not need to be further handicapped by putting her on roller skates! I repeat: Samantha must have a one-to-one aide!"

On December 8th I received the following letter from the Supervisor of Special Education:

"The Director has requested that I acknowledge your letter of November 22, 1977 and let you know that we have been working with many alternatives to assist your daughter, Samantha Brown, here at Garfield School. Kathy H. will be planning with me in the morning on one possibility. Also the Director has another possibility which we will be sharing with you very soon. You will be hearing from us within the week with more concrete information.

With reference to the note you received from Mrs. Olson, yes, this is a method of teaching that is proving to be effective and certainly not the beginning of Samantha's being put aside."

On December 10th I got another note from Mrs. Olson: "Great news! Your letter was very effective! The Director is trying to release funds from the county in order to pay for Sam's aide. It looks good. What we are going to do is write up specific reasons why an aide for Sam is needed. We would like to send along a copy of your letter also if you don't mind. It looks very encouraging."

CHAPTER TEN

Family Trip to San Francisco

Christmas is approaching and Alan has invited us to go to San Francisco to meet his parents. I want to go, but remembering what a nightmare the trip from Michigan was for Samantha, I'm not sure it is a good idea. Still, she has made a lot of progress since then and she obviously likes Alan and his boys, so I decided to take the chance on her behavior.

Alan's vehicle is a 1954 Chevrolet Carryall that has two bench seats and a large cargo area in the back. Mark and Frank made a comfortable looking nest with sleeping bags and pillows back there and still had room for luggage and Christmas presents. Samantha and Andrea were buckled into the middle bench seats and surrounded with pillows and blankets so they could sleep comfortably. We left at 4 a.m. – just popped them in the Carryall with their pajamas on. Samantha traveled very well for the first 150 miles, wide awake, then fussed and cried for the next 150 until she went to sleep.

Alan's parents turned out to be wonderful people, very warm and welcoming. I felt comfortable with them right away. Their home was awesome. It was perched high on a hill and looked like a one-story house. On the back side it dropped four levels down the side of the hill. From the kitchen window one could look down on the Golden Gate Bridge. There was a large livingroom on the top level that had lots of windows and decks. The entrance level had a comfortable-looking den furnished with leather furniture, the master bedroom and bathroom and at the far end of that area was the kitchen. Alan's room was the next level down and was rustic looking with knotty pine paneling. The bottom level was the laundry room and a workshop.

Mark and Frank ran off to visit with friends they had made on previous visits to Grandma and Grandpa's house and promised to be back for lunch. The rest of us settled in the livingroom and chatted, with Alan catching them up on happenings since the last time he had seen them.

Samantha was intrigued with all the stairs and kept going up and down without holding onto rails. Alan's Mom worried about that at first until she saw how adroitly Sam managed to do it. Sam had no difficulty adjusting to a strange house. Andrea was on her best behavior and mostly sat beside me.

Alan's Mom made sandwiches for lunch and after that the boys talked her into taking them to a shopping mall.

Sammie trying to get Andrea's attention

Meeting Alan's parents

Early in the evening, we all went out to dinner in an Italian restaurant. It was very crowded and I was afraid that Samantha would flip out with a tantrum and embarrass me. Alan was holding her in his arms and sat her beside him in the booth and she behaved beautifully.

When we got back to the house, Samantha and Andrea were both tired and we got them settled in bed in the den. The boys joined Grandma and Grandpa in front of the TV and Alan decided to show me some of his favorite places in San Francisco. We toured Fisherman's Wharf which was terribly crowded with tourists, then we drove up Powell Street where the cable cars run and watched them run down the hill with tourists hanging over the sides. We ended our tour by driving down Lombard Street, the crookedest street in The City.

The next morning Alan's Dad made waffles for breakfast and soon after that we loaded the Carryall and headed home. It had been a wonderful visit and, best of all, Samantha had behaved very nicely and made a good impression on Alan's folks.

Alan and I had a fully paid vacation from Santa Barbara Research Center between Christmas and New Years. We were in love with each other but neither of us were in any hurry to remarry. Our divorces had left scars that were barely healed and we both knew there were many pitfalls ahead in trying to merge a family with his two boys and my two girls. In the end, we decided to simply live together and see if we could make a go of it.

January 3, 1977, we moved into Alan's house. His house has four bedrooms. Mark and Frank each had their own rooms and Samantha and Andrea shared one.

In mid-January, Samantha finally got a one-to-one aide and the reports in her journal improved.

Sammie's Journal, January 11, 1977
Sue: I am so glad to hear that Sammie has a one-to-one aide! Now please discard the rollerskates. I do not approve of them in the classroom and Sam is still getting bruises on her knees and backside.

Teacher: The rain didn't help Sam's behavior. She was irritable and whining, but her programs went much more smoothly today.

CHAPTER ELEVEN

UCSB Autism Research Program

Alan and I have been asked to take part in a research program at the University of California at Santa Barbara. This is to be a four year study of how to teach autistic children. The first two years will be parent training to show us how we can teach Samantha. We received the following introduction to the program:

> "Many people have argued that autistic children cannot learn. This argument, however, appears to be in error. Autistic children can learn, but they only seem to do so if considerable care is taken in the learning situation. Autistic children do not seem to learn very much unless specific teaching rules, identified through research in the area of learning are closely followed. Slight deviations on the part of the teacher's teaching behavior produce major disruptions in the autistic child's learning. While it is obvious that there is still much to learn about the effective teaching of autistic children, there is currently a considerable amount of information known and published.

> WHAT WE OFFER:

> An intensive treatment program aimed at helping you manage the problems of your child which are currently of concern.

A treatment program in which you as parents take an active role in changing the behavior of your son or daughter.

A treatment approach that can be used for managing problems that may occur in the future.

Because of the numerous hours parents spend with their children, it is our belief that parents can have a great deal to do with changing child behavior. So it has been our approach over the past several years to work with parents and teach them how to do the things which will enable autistic children to learn.

It has been our experience (working with autistic children) that families we have worked with and have trained have been able to learn the principles of changing behavior, and the parents have done an excellent job in working directly with their autistic children. A trained therapist is assigned to work closely with each family throughout the training process. Treatment generally requires about one year for the referred child's behavior to show considerable improvement.

Parent training is accomplished through: (a) reading general texts; (b) reading manuals; (c) viewing videotape examples, and (d) feedback sessions. The specifics of treatment procedures will be discussed in more detail later. It should be kept in mind that although the chances for marked improvement are quite good, improvement in the child's behavior cannot be guaranteed.

WHAT WE REQUIRE:

Treatment at the Autism Parent-Training Project is somewhat demanding of a family in terms of both time and energy. During the course of treatment, the parents will be asked to carry out certain tasks which involve them collecting information or data for the therapist about their family. Data is, in a sense, the key word of our treatment procedure, because it allows the therapist to understand what is happening in the family and also allows both the therapist and the family to evaluate whether or not treatment is having an effect on the child's behavior. This data is collected in a number of different ways:

Parents fill out forms here during an office interview.

We will periodically send trained observers into your home to collect data at various points before, during, and after treatment.

You as parents may be asked to collect data on some particular problem behavior once treatment has begun"

The Team Leader who was assigned to Samantha is Glen D. He will be observing her during her classwork to determine a baseline for the project.

In order for Samantha to be included in the Autism Research Project, it was necessary for her to be evaluated by an outside source. An appointment was made for her to be observed and tested at the University of California at Los Angeles in their Neuro-Psychiatric Institute. I was informed of the appointment on Friday and she is to be there on Monday.

This Saturday is Alan's parents 50th wedding anniversary and there will be a large gathering of relatives in Fresno. His Dad has four brothers and three sisters and they will all be there along with spouses and children, so they have hired a hall and will serve dinner. We (all six of us) will be joining them. Fresno is about 90 miles East of us. It was fun meeting all those relatives and, of course, they were all interested in Alan's new additions to his family. One uncle, in particular, Uncle Lou had traveled from Kansas. He took a great interest in Samantha, carried her around the hall, gave her cookies and held her on his lap while he was talking with his brothers and sisters. It was apparently mutual admiration because Samantha seemed also delighted with him. There was a U-shaped table in the middle of the room with Alan's Dad and Mom seated in the middle. Uncle Lou was on the left side of the grouping and we were seated on the right. We had Samantha seated between us. Alan did or said something to correct Samantha (neither of us can even remember what it was) and Uncle Lou jumped up from his seat and stalked all the way around that table. He shook his finger in Alan's face and said, "You leave her alone! You hear me?" Alan, being the gentleman that he is, said, "Yes, sir, Uncle Lou!"

The following morning we all (Alan, me, Mark, Frank. Sammie and Andrea) piled into the Carryall and headed down Interstate 5 to Anaheim. Samantha was howling, obviously not happy to be back on the road. I said to Alan, "Do you suppose it's alright to correct her now! Uncle Lou can't hear us, can he?" Alan and the boys all laughed!

We found out later that Uncle Lou traveled back to Kansas, sat down in his favorite chair and died.

Alan dropped Sammie and me off at my sister Peggy's house in Anaheim and drove back home to Goleta. Peggy had lived in Los Angeles long enough to become completely familiar with the freeway system, so she would drive Samantha and me to our appointments at NPI. We were scheduled for three 2-hour appointments over the next three days. Samantha was taken into a small room with two people, grad-students, I presume. One worked with Sam with bead stringing, puzzles, matching shapes, etc., and the other took notes. Samantha alternated between cooperating and crying and throwing her body around. Peggy and I watched all this from behind a one-way window outside the room. When Sam cried, Peggy cried. Over the three days, they tested her cognitive ability and her motor ability. Their report was sent directly to Dr. K. and I never saw it. Samantha, however, was admitted to the Autism Project at UCSB, so I presumed that they had agreed that she was indeed autistic.

CHAPTER TWELVE .

Sammie Meets Glen

<u>January 13, 1978 -</u> Samantha began working with Glen both at Garfield School and the university. He found her journal useful for coordination between her school classes, her time at the university, Kids-N-Things and home.

After her first session at the university, Sam spent a quiet afternoon, went to bed at 7 pm and slept until 12:30 am. Then she exploded into hyperactivity, all but climbing the walls of her bedroom. Part of her wakefulness included shouting a variety of her word-sounds "da-dee, ba-ba-ba, etc. At 4:30 am I finally laid down in her bed with her and made her stay quiet long enough to go back to sleep.

<u>January 24, 1978: Glenn's First Journal Entry</u>
Glen: Sam is doing well in clinic. She is performing gross motor imitations and is getting less irritated. She also has "a" as in "baa" regularly and "ai" as in "hi" much of the time. We need a list of words that would be most functional for Sam if she could say them. These would be the ones we would work on first. She was tired and <u>very</u> grouchy today – eyes closing, lots of whining, etc.

Sue: Samantha is trying out another new word. She is saying "done". "Done" with breakfast, "done" with hair washing, "done" with hair dryer. She's very consistent now with "night-night" and with waving hi and bye.

<u>February 10, 1978</u> – My journal entry: Alan and I are getting married in

Las Vegas this weekend. Sammie is getting a super-terrific Daddy! She and I are <u>very</u> fortunate!

The way this came about was that Alan's Mom and Dad came for a visit awhile ago. His Mom said to him, "How long is this shakedown cruise going to last?" referring to the fact that we had been living together for a year. After they left, Alan and I began to talk about the possibility of getting married.

"You know", he said, "there is a big gun show in Las Vegas next weekend. Several of our club members will be there. We could go to the gun show and then round up a couple of the members as witnesses and get married there."

That sounded good to me so we called his folks and told them that if they would like to come down to Goleta and babysit, we could go to Vegas and get married.

We flew to Las Vegas, we met our friends, we wandered through the gun show exhibits, and around 11 pm we ended up in the Clark County Clerk's office where he performed a brief marriage ceremony. Afterwards our two witnesses wanted to celebrate, but Alan and I were dead tired. We went back to our room in the hotel and crashed. Both of us were asleep in about 2 minutes.

<u>April 21, 1978</u>. It is Samantha's 7th birthday. Her new grandparents gave her a big, springy rocking horse and she loves it. Alan had decided to make sure that Sam understood birthdays, candles, and presents. Every morning of the week before her birthday, he put a candle in a muffin, lit it and set it on the table in front of her. Then we all sang "Happy Birthday" and told her to blow out the candle. When the real day arrived and a real birthday cake was set in front of her, she blew out the candles and gave everybody a big smile!

Samantha was still wearing diapers. We all (her teachers, her aides, Alan and I) had been valiantly trying to toilet train her with very little success. Glen D. decided to make it the highest priority on his list. He rounded up about 10 volunteers at the university to cover her every waking moment. Alan and I would be the home team, of course. He provided the following guidelines for everybody.

TOILET TRAINING SAMMIE

The approach described below is intended to toilet train Sammie in all settings from morning until bedtime. It is designed to teach Sammie proper use of the toilet in the context of her regular daily activities at home, school, clinic and Kids N' Things. In order to be successful the approach must be implemented consistently by everybody concerned and all eliminations must be consequated immediately. The strategy is composed of three general components:

A. Frequent, Scheduled Toiletings – to provide many opportunities for successful use of toilet
B. Consequences for Successful Use of Toilet – rewards will be offered whenever Sammie goes in the toilet
C. Consequences for Accidents – all accidents will be consequated immediately with the "positive practice" procedures described below
D. Each of the components is described in detail below
E. Going to the Toilet – instruct Sammie to "go potty" approximately once every half-hour.
    1. Present instruction ("Sammy go potty")
    2. Prompt her to pat her bladder region with her right hand. This will be used by Sammie to signal a need to go at school and at other times when she is involved in activities.
    3. Follow her to bathroom – providing minimal guidance if she wanders astray.
    4. Provide minimal guidance for her to lower pants and sit on toilet.
    5. After approximately five minutes (or after she voids in toilet), offer minimal guidance for Sammie to rise from toilet, raise pants, wipe herself (if appropriate), flush toilet, etc.
F. Voiding in Toilet – enthusiastically reward Sammie for any voiding in toilet (use praise, hugs, tickles, edibles and/or whatever she might want most at the time); then, use minimal guidance to ensure that she completes toileting steps.
G. Accidents – all accidents will be detected with the assistance of the pants alarm (a buzzer that detects moisture). It is critical that all accidents be consequated immediately as follows:
    6. Firmly admonish Sammie by holding her shoulders (to insure attending) and saying, "No, you wet your pants!"

7. Guide Sammie to toilet using firm prompts to insure that she moves quickly and directly to the bathroom.

8. Prompt Sammie to change her pants (use guidance to make sure that she does this quickly and efficiently) and say, "You wet your pants; now you have to practice."

9. Require Sammie to proceed through entire toileting sequence – initiating the sequence from the point where accident occurred – at least 5 times. The sequence goes as follows: walk to bathroom, lower pants, sit on toilet for only about 5 seconds, stand, raise pants, return to place of accident. During practice, offer the amount of guidance necessary to move through the steps quickly and efficiently, while still allowing her to do as much of it as she can (or will). During practice, the trainer should adopt a matter-of-fact, non-punishing and non-rewarding attitude and demeanor.

Sammie is already capable of executing most of the toileting steps by herself. Therefore, minimal guidance should be used for most of the above toileting activities. The one exception is positive practice where guidance should be sufficiently firm for Sammie to proceed through the sequence efficiently and rapidly."

Thus was launched what we came to refer to as "The Fire Brigade"! Alan and I began the procedure by putting her on the potty every half hour and following all of the above steps. When it was time for her to go to school, two of the volunteers would pick her up at our house in their cars and rush her off. They had practiced the run in advance and scouted out places where they could stop (gas stations, etc.) in case Samantha indicated that she needed to go potty. The teacher and aides took over at school by putting her on the potty as soon as she got there and every half hour after that. A second team of volunteers drove her to Kids N' Things and repeated the procedure every half hour until I picked her up at 5 pm.

In less than a month's time, Samantha was toilet trained and graduated to regular panties. She still had occasional bowel movement accidents for about another month and then she began having total toileting success.

CHAPTER THIRTEEN

Results/Improvements within the Autism Program

In late April there was a Parent Advisory Meeting called by the Director of Special Education that I was unable to attend because I was flat in bed with pneumonia. Mrs. Olson did attend and wrote the following note in Samantha's journal:

"At the meeting last night, parents from Goleta were confused and concerned about a form they received asking them to sign their child into Goleta's program. Not all of their questions were answered, but a few things were explained. Some Goleta parents feel that their desire to mainstream their child by placing him on a regular campus is a top priority. Goleta has lost so many children (with he closure of Hollister Autism Project) they need more to fill programs. Parents in Goleta want the children from Garfield to start a new program. Other parents don't like the idea of mainstreaming and asked if they had to do this. The Director said he would not force parents from Garfield to Goleta but transportation problems might make such a change inevitable. That is, if enough children go to Goleta, the cost of having bus service for one or two children to Garfield would be pretty expensive. I would suggest that in finding out about the Goleta program you ask (among other things) if a speech therapist, sensory motor specialist, and a physical therapist would be available as they are at Garfield. Class size, number of aides, size of school would also be concerns."

I didn't hear anything more about this until I received a letter from the Director written May5, 1978.

"Mrs. Brown: I would like to take this opportunity, in my continuing communication with you, to welcome you to the Severely Handicapped Programs in the Goleta Union School District.

I can appreciate the many concerns you might have relative to this transition and would like to invite you to a meeting on Tuesday, May 16, at El Rancho School, 7:30 pm, in the Kindergarten Pod. At this meeting, I would like to discuss the general philosophy of programs for the Severely Handicapped and would appreciate your input in order to organize our programs for summer and September of 1978.

Your attendance at this meeting is vitally important, not only for the organization of our programs for this summer and September, but also it is important in order to meet your teacher and other support personnel."

On May 18, 1978, I wrote this letter to him:

"Alan and I enjoyed meeting you on the 16th of May and discussing your program for Severely Handicapped children.

As I stated at that meeting, I will be continuing to send Samantha to Garfield School for the coming summer session and the 1978-79 school year. Her program is all arranged with Garfield, with a very ambitious objective already agreed up and ready to put into action.

We will, however, keep in touch with your program and are interested in its development."

On the 20th of May, I wrote in Sam's journal after a conference at Garfield: "Good conference yesterday! Your programs, persistence, and cooperation have done wonderful things for Sammie. I'm grateful to all of you and I'm glad it has worked out so that Sam has at least another year at Garfield."

That same day when I arrived at Kids N' Things to pick up Samantha, Marnie had her sitting at a table with other little girls, coloring with crayons. Now that was truly "mainstreaming" and a chance for Sam to get used to normal children in a different setting,

One of the grad students at UCSB who was working on his doctorate in audiology asked if we would allow him to test Samantha's hearing. Of course, we said yes. He found that her hearing was perfect in her left ear, but in the right ear the signal would get lost before it reached the auditory portion of her brain. Coincidentally, she has always slapped that ear! Since she cannot talk, there is no way of knowing what she is hearing in her right ear.

May 25, 1978 – Note in Sam's journal from me: "When the bus didn't pick Sam up on Monday, I took her to school and I noticed a remarkable thing. As soon as Sam was on campus, she began "autistic behaviors" I have not seen at home for months! I was surprised when you (teacher) mentioned tantruming earlier in this journal, but after seeing her turn on her hand-flapping, stiff-legged, uncooperative attitude, I am beginning to understand. I need to mention it to Glen and then perhaps we need to get together to discuss what to do about the problem."

UCSB AUTISM PROJECT

Client: Samantha Brown
Clinical Treatment: 2-78 to 3-79
Clinicians: Glen, Jill, Lynn

Learning Readiness

When Sam was first in clinic she exhibited many behaviors that were not condusive to a clinical setting. Among these behaviors were tantruming ranging from five minutes to over an hour, wetting her pants, and high self-stimulation levels. Decreasing these behaviors was an overall clinical goal. Time out was found to be ineffective. Within a few months Sam's tantruming had decreased to negligible levels. This was achieved by ignoring the tantrum and continuing to present instructions (such as "Touch your head.")

In May, after several previous attempts, an intensive toilet training program began. This involved using buzzer pants and positive practice. It involved precise coordination between home, UCSB clinic and school. By mid-June Sam had almost 100% success with urine at school and home. Bowel movements took longer (until December) for complete success. Presently Sam is completely toilet trained and able to self initiate.

During clinic Sam's self stim was so high it was interfering with her ability to attend and respond. In August suppression of vocal stim began. The therapist briskly held her hand over Sam's mouth. Vocal stim was effectively decreased from 85%-90% of the time intervals to approximately 60% of the intervals. In September total suppression began. A light, but brisk slap on her hand and a stern "no" were used for suppression; additionally it seemed important to provide her with challenging tasks which interest ed and with reinforcement for no self stim. Her stim in clinic ranged from 15 to 65%, consistently lower than presuppression data. Anecdotally, suppression increased eye contact compliance and attention.

Specific Clinic Tasks

During Sam's year in clinic we worked on various tasks. She successfully acquired many of them. One of her strong areas was gross motor imitation. She would generally respond between 80 to 90% correct. Her acquired responses included: clapping, touching her head with one and two hands, clapping hands above her head, raising one and two arms, putting arms out horizontally, crossing her arm to touch her opposite shoulder, stamping her feet, touching her feet, standing up, turning around, and jumping.

Various sorting skills were worked on. She could successfully (90%) sort red, blue and white poker chips. Between 60 to 80% of the time she correctly matched four to five wooden numbers. When the task became more difficult, by using more complex stimuli, such as a card with one circle versus two circles, she seemed to concentrate more and did equally well on the task. Sam could also match pictures of a comb, ball and toothbrush to the objects 75 to 80% of the time. When given the instruction "feet" or "head" she could correctly touch the appropriate body part 80% of the time. We worked on sign language for about three weeks and during that time she acquired the expressive and receptive use of three signs: food, water, and play dough.

Other tasks we worked on presented Sam with more difficulty. A basic imitation paradigm was used for speech. We worked on two phonemes, (m) and (a). She would reach criterion on one sound and then the other but she never expressively discriminated between the two sounds. Another area of difficulty was the identification of common objects. If two objects were presented she could learn both of them but when the order became random frequently so did her responding. These were two main areas of difficulty.

Additional Self Help Skills

Throughout the clinic treatment additional self help skills were also included in the curriculum. Sam learned to put on her jacket without prompts if it was handed to her the right way (held at the shoulders with the sleeves inside out). Sam can also pick it up from the table or chair and put it on correctly if the sleeves are not inside out. Occasionally she gets an arm in the wrong sleeve and at that she requires prompting. She can put on a tee-shirt if it is held in the right direction, without manual prompts. Occasionally a verbal prompt such as "put in your arm" was used. Sam worked on putting on her pants during toilet training. She can pull up her pants and zip them but she needs manual prompt to help her snap them. Sam can put on her shoes if the right and left shoes are on the correct sides and pull the laces tight. She needs verbal prompting and also at times manual prompts to keep her on task. She can turn on the faucet, wash her hands, turn off the faucet and dry her hands with minimal manual prompts. With guidance, Sam can put a toothbrush in her mouth and stroke approximately seven times. We also worked on Sam's eating habits. The two basic problems were that she ate too fast and stimmed while food was in her mouth. We worked on this by cutting her sandwich into quarters and placing one section in front of her at a time. She had to place the section down after every bite. Her left hand was not to be used and remained on the table. Verbal prompts were primarily used with some manual guidance until she was eating nicely without self stimming.

Overall Improvements

Sam has improved greatly in the areas of social behavior and receptive language. In such situations as eating in restaurants and sitting quietly in cars, she is much more enjoyable to be around. She shows increasing awareness of people around her and demonstrates this by crying and wanting affection when she falls down and hurts herself, laughing when tickled and demanding attention by pulling people to what she is interested in. Further, she shows a great interest in learning now and appears more motivated to work on more challenging tasks. We expect to see continued and possibly more rapid progress because of this.

Parent Training

Sam and her parents recently started work in the parent training part of the UCSB Autism Project. Her parents have both shown high levels of skill in dealing with Sam before training. The training has helped to refine their skills. They are both highly motivated to work with Sam and this should aid Sam's progress. They are currently working on speech a great deal, as well as discriminations and other tasks. Further training and their continued dedication should yield good progress with Sam.

Social Behaviors

Sam has steadily improved during the past 12-15 months. This was demonstrated on video tapes taken in her home and at UCSB. Sam and her family were filmed together while eating dinner. Over the year, she showed improvement by acquiring certain appropriate dinner time behaviors. By looking at the video tapes at the end of her involvement in the clinical portion of our project, Sam did not exhibit disruptive behavior as she did when she first started.

The video tapes done at our clinic were filmed while Sam was interacting with her parents and clinician. Sam and each individual adult were filmed through a one-way mirror while interacting in a room decorated as a "living room", filled with toys. By comparing the tapes over the year period, we saw a decrease in inappropriate behaviors such as self-stimulation, tantrums, and general non-cooperation. We also saw an increase in appropriate behaviors while interacting with the adults in such areas as appropriate play, cooperation and appropriate interaction initiated by Sam.

End of Report

The video tapes mentioned above by Glen (in the Social Behavior section) were an interesting family event. Our reactions ran the gamut from being self-conscious, embarrassed, giggling, not being able to carry on a normal conversation. Can you imagine trying to get through a family meal with 3 extra people with video cameras, lights, and tape recorders? One of our neighbors/friend had no problem at all with the concept. The second time the team came in we were about halfway through the meal when Bill walked in, sat down at the table, and started telling a funny story about his day!

CHAPTER FOURTEEN

Annual Review –
Tri-Counties Regional Center

We also received a report from Kathy H. dated 2-8-79:

ANNUAL REVIEW

I. IDENTIFYING INFORMATION

Samantha Jo Brown will be 8 in April. Samantha's natural parents are divorced. She is residing with her mother and stepfather and sibling in Goleta. Samantha is involved in a full time school program at Garfield School. Vi Olson and Bonnie Robinson are her principal teachers. She has a full time aide, Robin Ross funded through the school. Childcare arrangements have been made for Samantha at Kids N Things by Mrs. Brown, who is employed on a full time basis at Santa Barbara Research. Because of Samantha's need for supervision in this setting on a one-to-one basis, an aide has been funded for two hours per day five days per week through United Health Care Services by Tri-Counties Regional Center.

II. FAMILY SITUATION

Samantha's mother and stepfather are actively concerned about her welfare and her mother is an active participant in the development of programming for Samantha.

III. CURRRENT FUNCTIONING

A. Motor Domain: Samantha is an agile little girl who has always had good gross motor ability. She has no difficulty with walking and running and has learned to rollerskate on the sidewalk at school as well. Her fine motor skills age good and she is an exceptionally quick child who is believed to have perceptual problems. Her difficulties with planning and sequencing inter-fere with her ability to complete gross and fine motor tasks. Her teachers report that Samantha is now able to rollerskate on a definite inside route in the Garfield School area, stop and return on her own. In the past, Samantha has had a tendency to run off if not directly supervised. The occupational therapist has reported that Samantha seems to respond to rough tactile stimulation. She likes her arms and legs rubbed and her back scratched. Although her mother reports that she has begun to carry around a piece of satin at home, in the school environment she has not yet displayed an interest in smooth objects. They are working with her using the net and swing. The objective is to have Samantha do a task and complete it. She is now able to swing on her stomach for four minutes, fifteen seconds (first try) and six minutes on the second try. She usually is rewarded with a back rub. Vision problems are improving but still exist. Mrs. Brown feels that she has better peripheral than straight vision especially at a distance.

B. Communicative Domain: Samantha is felt to have good expres-sive and receptive non-verbal communication as well as to be receptively able to understand the meaning of simple conversa-tion and a combination of verbal instructions. When utilized, her expressive language consists of simple one syllable sounds used in association with appropriate objects. Most individuals, including her speech therapist, have indicated some surprise when they have heard Samantha speak because she speaks so seldom. She only uses language, according to her mother, when in a situation which she regards as an emergency. Samantha does have some receptive and expressive sign language. These are signs specifically developed for her.

C. Social Domain: Samantha is able to initiate interaction in fa-miliar or previously successful situations or settings. She also initiates interaction with persons other than peers. Potential friends must initiate friendships and the maintenance of friendships occurs only in stable or familiar settings. Samantha participates in social activities with some encouragement and participates in group projects but her efforts do not contribute to the group effort. At this point, unacceptable social behaviors seldom interfere with social participation. Most of Samantha's interaction in the school setting is with her aide, Robin Ross, with whom she seems to have formed a close relationship. Her teachers report that she is beginning to become more aware of other children on the playground and recently said "stop" when one child began pulling her hair.

D. <u>Emotional Domain</u>: Samantha has made considerable gains over the last year. Episodes of self-injurious behavior do not occur more than three times a year and when the behavior occurs, no apparent injury takes place. Samantha seems to be exercising more control with supervision. She will stop an activity, such as rollerskating, within a specified limit. Episodes of destruction of property have decreased to once during the past year, and this was minor in nature. Her mother feels that there is no evidence of depressive-like behavior and that Samantha deals effectively with frustrating situations. Repetitive body movements occur only under conditions of excitement and/or stress and Samantha no longer undresses herself inappropriately. Without one-on-one supervision, however, Samantha is hyperactive. Temper tantrums have decreased to one per month or less. She is resistive only in stressful situations.

E. <u>Cognitive Domain</u>: Although Samantha is felt to have perceptual problems, it is felt that she can recognize words that sound the same and respond differently to objects based on differences of color, size and shapes. She does associate regular events with a specific hour. She counts by rote, and is presently working on obtaining an understanding of the concepts of 1,2,3 and 4. Her mother feels she has some pre-writing skills in that she is able to copy from a model or trace. She has no reading skills but is working on matching the letters A,B and C. She is now able to focus on a single activity between five and fifteen minutes. Her safety awareness is low in that she requires supervision on a daily basis in order to prevent situations in which she puts herself into dangerous positions. She is able to display her memory of instructions or demonstrations if they are repeated three or more times and she is prompted to recall.

Her teachers feel that she has met educational objectives in that she is now able to string beads, including small ones. Different colors have been added in order to reach her color patterns. She has increased her receptive and expressing language. She can sort numbers from one to three and match the set two numbers. She has increased her attention span to between one and five minutes. Her self-image has improved in that she now looks in a mirror, both her face and her total self. Previously she used to withdraw.

F. Independent living Domain: Samantha is now able to go to the toilet by herself but needs assistance to complete toileting. She has complete bladder and bowel control. Her eating has now improved to the point where she is able to feed herself using a fork and spoon with spillage. She is able to tend to some personal hygiene needs but not complete. She is able to participate in bathing but since she has problems with determining hot and cold, does not run her own bath water. She puts some clothes on by herself and cooperates in putting on clothes in general. She is beginning to complete household chores and does participate in food preparation, bedmaking and washing dishes. She is not involved in money handling, making purchases or ordering food in public.

HEALTH/MEDICAL STATUS

Samantha has fairly good health. Her illnesses are mainly minor colds. She is not taking any ongoing medications. Here dental health appears to be good.

End of Report

The "emergency language" Kathy referred to occurred when she almost set the house on fire. Alan had been trying to get her to say "Daddy, up" in the mornings when she came into our room. Early one morning I heard her call from the kitchen "Daddy, up" and I jumped up to congratulate her on talking. She had turned on a gas burner on the stove and then waved a dish towel in the flame. She dropped the flaming towel on the floor and yelled for Daddy! Fortunately, the incident resulted in only a small scorched spot in the linoleum. She was also able to say "hot" if I ran her bath water too hot.

I was curious about Samantha's activities at school and I asked Robin to give me an hour-by-hour rundown of a typical day. She responded with this report:

April 16, 1979

8:45-9:00--Potty – Samantha urinated in toilet. She asked to ride rocking horse with her sign for ride. She rode for a few minutes then went to record player and picked up head phones. She listened to music after giving her sign for music (hands over ears). She was very quiet. Rocked in her chair.

9:00-9:30—Morning circle. She tapped her knees in time to our good morning song with only 3 or 4 prompts from me. She did appropriate hand movements to our number song.

She participated in taking down our Easter bunny by taking down his yellow shoes on command from Mrs. Arnold. Then we worked with the three bears. Sam picked up the Papa bear. Lots of jumping up from her chair, spinning around, and spitting.

9:30-10:00 – Sam is in speech with therapist.

10:00-10:30 – Receptive language. Three objects are put on a table. Today it was shirt, book, toy. Sam sits five feet away. Teacher says "Sammie, give me _____." Sam is to stand up retrieve article, show what it is to be used for. "Sam, what do you do with it." (shirt – hold it up to front, book – open it up and flip pages, toy - play with it). Sam's score today: shirt – one correct out of four, book – three correct out of six, toy – three out of 8. This is not up to par for Sam. She was a bit "spacey". Lots of kicking.

10:30-11:00 – Potty. Snack. Sam gave sign for apple with a prompt from teacher. Play time – Sam spends most of her time in the bushes, pulling leaves off trees and rubbing sticks and other debris in her palms. However, she is becoming increasingly aware of the playground equipment and especially the merry-go-round.

11:00-11:30 – Sam worked on brushing her teeth. Toothbrush on table. "Sam, brush your teeth". Sam picked up toothbrush, brushed her teeth, put it down. She did very well. Sam also worked on her sign for scratch. Teacher: "Do you want a scratch?" Sam gives her sign (fingers brush the palm of other hand) and then she gets a scratch. She did very well on this, too.

11:30 – Potty. Lunch time. Sam waited in line as patiently as possible for her. Lots of fidgeting and swaying, jumping and playing with the wall, but she kept her place in line. On command, she gets her tray, spoon and straw with help from teacher. Then she pushes tray and gets milk and carries tray to the table on her own. Today she wasn't paying attention very well so she needed 3-4 prompts to complete the sequence. She needs monitoring for tipping and placement of her tray. Multiple prompts are necessary to get consistency in eating with spoon. Without supervision off task behaviors include: eating with fingers, tearing food and self stimming with it, sticking other children, taking food from other trays, making noise, swinging feet striking table, tapping tray on table, tapping spoon on table, tapping spoon on tray, standing up on bench, leaving lunch area. With supervision she is responsive to verbal directions to delete, redirect, modify her behavior. Potty – Sam jumping up and down, twirling.

12:15-1:00 – Play time. Due to weather, we played inside. Sam played mostly in bean bag chair and in front of mirror.

1:00-1:30 – Sam did a series of tasks in sequence: (1) string 5 large beads; (2) 5-piece puzzle; (3) sort 3 colors (blocks); (4) 4 piece fruit puzzles. She did two tasks in 3 minutes and it took 17 prompts to keep her on task. To give you some idea as to how she did, she has worked up to 3 tasks in 3 minutes, and her approximate average is 9 prompts per 3 tasks.

1:30-2:00 – Sam rollerskates in the courtyard. We have a beach ball almost as big as Sam and she pushes it around as she skates. Today she stayed involved for 5 minutes at a time.

2:00-2:30 – Sam swings in the net swing in a prone position and spins herself. She loves to swing this way now as she can maneuver herself with her arms.

Next, I rolled the bolster over her front and back like a rolling pin. This calms her down. She especially likes this on her back.

Then we use the blindfold (this in itself makes her very quiet) and rub her body with different textures. Today I used the loofa and a soft furry fabric. She liked the fabric best and showed it by being very quiet and relaxed. Sometimes this relaxes her so much she falls asleep. This is done in the bean bag chair.

2:30-2:45 – Potty. Get ready for bus. Say "bye".

September 12, 1979 Journal Notes
Sue: I can't begin to tell you how happy Sam will be to be back in school! Her past couple of weeks have been boring for her. She's doing great with our home speech therapy sessions. We've been quite successful in getting her to say both "Mama" and "Daddy". In the university parent-training program, she's doing very well at distinguishing colors (red, yellow, blue) and shapes (circle, square, triangle).

Mrs. Olson: Sam had a wonderful first day at school. She was obviously pleased to see Robin (aide). We got several verbal responses from her and her noises seem closer to true sounds as they relate to speech. Today's task performance shows good retention of skills but length of on task behavior has regressed.

CHAPTER FIFTEEN

Personal Stories

<u>September 18, 1979</u> AUTISTIC CHILD : This is a story written by Samantha's older sister, Karen, for a college class in Journalism:

"As a baby, Sammie preferred not to be handled and cried when touched," says her mother, Sue Brown. "She wouldn't reach out in anticipation of being picked up – there was no response, she just stared at you."

"I became concerned when Sammie was about eight months old," continues Sue, "She was so withdrawn and wasn't mimicking, but her motor development was normal."

"When Sammie was 18 months old, she didn't want to be in the same room with people" remembers Sue, "and her tantrums were increasing and becoming more violent."

"Sammie has banged her head through several walls, without any sign of pain," her mother says, "and she was always scratching and digging herself."

Moving from Michigan to California was particularly traumatic to Sammie, who has trouble adjusting to changes, and her scratching tantrums led to a blood stream infection.

"I had to pin socks to her clothes, covering her hands, until her face healed", mentioned Sue.

As a pre-schooler, Sammie did not play with toys or other children. She had not yet learned to talk. Samantha Jo Brown is an autistic child.

Autistic children are unresponsive to their environment. They do not play with toys or other children. They show no need for any form of contact with anybody. They often throw violent screaming tantrums. Many are happiest when left alone.

There is no proof yet of what causes autism. One theory places the blame on the parents emotional problems which somehow cause the child's tragic withdrawal. This theory only reinforces the guilt the parents already mistakenly feel.

"For a long time I kept thinking if I hadn't done this, or maybe if I hadn't taken Sammie there … " Sue says tearfully, "maybe this wouldn't have happened".

A more current theory is looking at organic disorders as the cause of autism. While this theory may help relieve the parent guilt, it does not offer any solutions.

Sammie was three weeks old when she was hospitalized for meningitis (inflammation of the membranes of the brain or spinal cord). It had started out with a low fever (99 degrees) and then Sammie went into convulsions.

Sammie's hospital stay lasted three weeks. During that time, she had many painful tests performed, including several spinal taps. Sammie was fed intravenously through her right hand (which she now continually bites during tantrums).

Sue believes Sammie's problems can be traced back to this early illness. As the mother of four normal children, she cannot really accept the parental blame theory.

Sammie is an agile, fair-skinned blond-haired little girl. She lives with her sister, mother, step-father and two step-brothers in Goleta, California. She has two older half-sisters and one half-brother who live elsewhere. Sue works full-time at Santa Barbara Research Center as an Administrative Secretary.

Sammie, now 8 years old, has been in several educational programs since she was two years old. She currently attends Garfield School. She became involved in a research program at the UCSB Autism Laboratory, under the direction of Dr. K.

The UCSB Autism Laboratory represents a joint function of the Speech and Hearing Center and the Social Process Research Institute. The faculty and students conduct research on the understanding and treatment of autistic children.

Through behavior modification techniques (systematically rewarding appropriate behavior while ignoring or punishing inappropriate behavior) the program has achieved some lasting improvements.

"Getting Sammie potty-trained is one of the major benefits we've received through the program", claims Sue. "It took an all-out concentrated program. The students at the university were terrific. They would take turns taking Sam to school rather than having her ride the bus and risk an 'accident'", continues Sue, "the training continued regardless of where she was 24 hours a day."

Sammie's parents are involved in a parent-teaching program, too. Dr. K. says, "The parents participation in the treatment process is essential. Excluding the parents wastes a valuable and necessary resource.

Behavior modification techniques are easily taught to non-professionals and considerable improvements are achieved. Literally every activity becomes a learning experience for the child because of the continuous treatment.

We do not claim to be able to cure autism," states Dr. K, "and some autistic children may never be completely normal. But we have found that all can achieve significant progress."

The next major goal for Sammie is communication development. Sammie is currently learning sign language, which will help her communicate her needs to others. She understands simple conversation and responds to commands. Sammie can speak a few words, but mainly uses them when in a situation which she regards as an emergency, claims her mother.

"Sometimes I get the feeling that Sammie knows what she wants to say, and wants to say it, but can't," describes Sue. "it's like aphasia – a stroke victim without the ability to speak."

Many of Sammie's frustrations are from communication problems. However, her tantrums have decreased to one per month or less, and self-injurious behavior occurs on rare occasions.

Sammie's attention span has improved during the past year and she is learning several matching tasks with letters and numbers and colors and shapes.

"Sammie is becoming aware of herself and people are no longer threatening to her", Sue states, obviously pleased. "She displays affection now – even initiates it!"

I don't view Sammie as a problem child. I see her as a happy, lovable child with some severe problems to overcome," asserts Sue. "She's not a burden to us!"

End of Story

<u>September 18, 1979</u>
Sue: On the weekend Alan was whistling along with a tune on the radio. Sam sat beside him, puckered up and blew. That's mimicking! That's new for her.

Robin: Yes! We've been noticing some imitative behavior here at school, too. This is very exciting! I was working with her on her expressive language and instead of saying "Sam, touch head", etc. I said "do this" and she did just great. Later I was looking in the mirror with her and moving my lips with no noise and she imitated my lip movements perfectly. Then she added her own noise to it.

Jill (clinician at UCSB): Sam was in a great mood today, laughing and giggling. She had an accident in her pants at the end of the day. After she got cleaned up she was able to put her pants on and her shoes on all alone. She can also pull her shoelaces tight. She was in a real social mood today; going up to other people and giving me lots of kisses! Sam's latest project is tying her shoes. She can tie a knot with very few prompts.

<u>September 19,1979</u>
Robin: Sam did a wonderful thing today in gross motor. She initiated a small game of catch with another child who was sitting close to her. The ball was just lying there and she was sort of kicking it around, then just rolled it to the other child. They kept it going back and forth for about 2 minutes.

<u>My Sammie Story</u>
I enrolled in a creative writing class at City College to try to prepare myself to write Samantha's story someday in the future. This is what I wrote for that class:

SAMANTHA

She is sitting here beside me now with her warm, small body pressed against me. It's another indication hat she's healing – I used to be included on her list of terrors to be avoided whenever possible. I look down at her small hand, her bony shoulders. I want to hold her hand (or at least touch it). I want to put my arm around her. But she would pull away like a small, frightened animal. So, instead, I sit very still, savoring the moment. There is a bond of love between us and I welcome this small sharing of it.

She's eight years old. Small for her age. Her seven year old sister is a full head taller. She looks delicate, fragile. She's pale and thin. Not unhealthy-looking, but ethereal; as though her body bears testimony to the difficulty of living in a world she doesn't comprehend. She's a beautiful child, with a round face, evenly-formed features, fine pale-blonde hair cut in a pixie-style cap. She has large, clear bright blue eyes framed by long, dark eyelashes. Those eyes. Sometimes she uses them with a gaze so direct and open that you can see behind them into her mind where her words are locked. Sometimes they are clouded with confusion – too much input, overloading the circuits that are not operating properly. Sometimes she uses them for "time out". It's a very familiar procedure. One I've seen countless times since she was a baby. Left hand, with fingers spread open, held in front of her face. Right hand with fleshy part between thumb and forefinger jammed into her mouth. Eyes focused intently on the palm of her left hand. "Go away, world! You frighten me! I'm safer in here."

Now that we understand, we say, gently, "Put your hand down, Sammie. You don't need it. You are OK." Because she trusts us, she puts her hand down and comes back into our world.

Birth itself is a trauma, say the experts. What then was it like for a three-week old baby, who had barely begun to experience love, to be thrust back into the hospital to spend twenty-one days suspended between life and death in excruciating pain. Pain from the pressure in her head; pain from the needles in her spine; and the needles that provided sustenance intravenously to keep her alive while they tore open her flesh every time she moved. Viral meningitis is not a rare disease, just difficult to define. One apparently either dies from it, or recovers completely.

"Ninety-nine out of a hundred cases have no after-effects whatsoever", said the pediatrician and he stuck with that opinion, calling me an over-anxious mother when I pointed out areas that weren't developing properly in my baby. For a long time I thought I could "love the hurt away". If I loved her enough, made her feel how much I loved her, she would be OK. But, as the parent of every handicapped child eventually learns, love is not enough.

The label for her condition is: Autistic. The prognosis: no cure. Some experts say, "As the child is at four, so shall he be at twenty-four". Those same experts have tried to blame the condition on lack of mother-love. But I know how much I love this child. And so I discount the rest of their learned pronouncements and search for the key to unlock the closed doors between my world and Samantha's. Hers was not a pleasant place – it was fearful and dark. It made her scream and bang her head on walls. It made her jab, bite and tear at her own body. But with love, patience and our stubborn determination not to lose her, she's come a million miles. Slowly and painfully. We measure her with a whole different yardstick than one usually applies to a child. Each small improvement is a milestone.

We have recently determined, through research conducted by a graduate student in audiology, that her hearing is perfect but that the brain waves become confused before they reach the cortex. This confirms our long-held suspicion that there might be a small lesion (scar tissue) in the auditory portion of her brain as a result of the many convulsions she suffered during her illness. Her speech development is almost nonexistent. In eight years, her only words are ones she uses in emergency: "hot" "eat" "bye-bye". She can mimic a seagull at the beach, or an ape at the San Francisco with amazing clarity. She will not mimic human beings. Is it because we represent pain and terror?

She's still sitting here beside me. If I can't touch her, I still want to try to express what I feel for her. Finally I say, very quietly, "I love you, Sammie."

No. That's too abstract for a little one who may have no understanding of "I" or "me". I change my words to, "Mommy loves you."

She stares down at the ground as though she might not have heard me. Then she begins a tentative "Da", followed by a sure, clear, "Da-dee". The word we have been working for in our home speech therapy sessions.

I say, "Oh, good talking, Sam! Good Da-dee!" She returns my wide smile with a small, shy one of her own. Then, with a mischievous, gleeful sparkle in those blue eyes, she says, softly "Mama".

I am reassured, once again, that one day my little girl will be well.

CHAPTER SIXTEEN

The Diagnostic School for Neurologically Handicapped Children

The following letter was received by the Director of Special Education on September 10, 1979, from the Superintendent of the Diagnostic School for Neurologically Handicapped Children, Southern California:

"The Diagnostic School for Neurologically Handicapped Children, Southern California, offers your district services to children with special needs that are unique and unparalleled in the State of California. These special services are offered to you through the State Department of Education. They include a five day evaluation by a team of educational diagnosticians, speech and language specialists, psychologists, and a pediatrician. Also offered to some children is a residential program that enables us to look more closely at the child in a full time educational setting. The main goal of the residential program is to develop further diagnostic information and then develop and organize recommendations for the remedial process. A follow-up person is also offered to you to help implement the findings and recommendations made by our evaluation team.

These services are provided to you, the child and his parents without charge. This includes room and board for the five day evaluation. When a child is selected for our short term residential, remedial education program, your school district will be responsible for the cost of education for the period the child is enrolled at the Diagnostic School. This shall not exceed the cost of educating a child in the local school district. The maximum length of stay for any child is one school year.

Referrals to the Diagnostic School must be made in writing by the designated administrators in your district, which notes that the district has exhausted its resources to provide services necessary to determine the student's educational needs. A letter which identifies the problems which interfere with the child's ability to learn, the specific reason(s) for referral to the Diagnostic School, the interventions which the school and community have attempted prior to referral is required. This letter must be accompanied by recent (within the last school year) psychological reports, speech and hearing reports, health reports (from the child's physician)."

Although I was unaware of this letter at that point in time, it had an unexpected impact for me. Dr. C. of Tri-Counties Regional Center ordered a CAT scan for Samantha as part of her health report for the referral. In doing so, he also contacted the hospital in Grand Rapids, Michigan, requesting their records of her three-week hospitalization when she was three weeks old. He contacted me to report the findings of the CAT scan (which showed several lesions in the top of her brain and atrophy at the lower edges). He said, "By the way, the hospital records said her illness was encephalitis, not meningitis."

I was stunned! Why hadn't they ever told me that? Encephalitis causes a swelling of the brain itself, not the outside covering of the brain! And, wait a minute, the most common cause of encephalitis is a mosquito bite. But she was born in April and Michigan doesn't have mosquitoes until later in the year. Suddenly and clearly, I remembered that horrible monkey that Roy's cousin had brought into the house. Monkeys are notorious flea carriers and fleas are known to be carriers of encephalitis! Samantha who was a normal, healthy baby, had been brought down by a flea!

<u>October 1, 1979</u>
Mrs. Olson: Sam was doing lots of hyperventilating today. A "Shh" or "stop" will stop it for a few seconds and then she is back at it.

Sue: We have been suppressing hyperventilating with a squirt bottle filled with water. You may have to do the same if it doesn't stop

<u>October 2</u>
Mrs. Olson: We used the squirt bottle some today. She is somewhat calmer. The squirt bottle is very effective.

<u>October 15</u>
Mrs. Olson: Samantha seems to have less need to abuse herself, but such a need for scratching/rubbing. It is painful to recognize the extremes she must go to in order to satisfy her need for sensory input. At these times Robin intensifies her adaptive PE program as it relates to "sensations".

I received the following letter from the Neuropsychiatric Institute (NPI) University of California, Los Angeles :

"Dear Parents:

Your child, Samantha, was seen at the UCLA-NPI and participated in a project which is seeking to objectively diagnose autism and follow the development of the child as he/she grows older. The purpose of the research project is to try to better understand your child's condition and help future children who receive the diagnosis of autism. In order to do this, it is necessary to periodically re-evaluate all the children and see how they are doing. Therefore, we are asking once again for your co-operation in bringing your child to UCLA.

If necessary, we would be able to pay you $6 to cover the cost of bringing your child to UCLA. There would be no charge to you. The appointment will, of course, be made at your convenience.

Thank you in advance for your cooperation.
Sincerely, B. J. F., Ph.D.
Assistant Professor of Medical Psychology"

I found the offer of $6 to cover the cost of this request somewhat ludicrous and responded as follows:

"Dear Dr. F.:

Samantha's and my last trip to NPI resulted in $250 out-of-pocket expense (as itemized below) and almost zero useable information for either myself or Dr. K.

I would love to have you re-evaluate Samantha because she has made great positive gains this year in UCSB's Autism Project. I would, therefore, like to make an alternative suggestion. Why don't you come to Santa Barbara? Dr. K. has assured me that he would make his facilities available at UCSB and I am sure you would find them excellent for your purpose. In addition, the students who regularly work with Sam could observe your data gathering techniques as well as give you additional scientific input as to her progress this past year.

Sincerely,
Suzanne C. Brown

My expenses for January 1977 evaluation at NPI
$150 – 3 days leave of absence without pay
$40.00 – gasoline for round trip (SB-LA-SB) made by my husband
$20.00 – gasoline used in daily trips to university
$40.00 – plane tickets for return to Santa Barbara
$250.00

October 26
Robin: This morning Sam had some free time and she went by herself over to the toy shelf and picked out the wooden doughnut toy, took it over to the table, sat down, and played with it. She took the doughnuts

off and put them back on 8-9 times taking at least that many minutes before moving on to something else.

Sue: She's playing with a big rag doll at home these days and repeated "doll" when Alan said it.

November 26
Robin: Sam and I had a rough day together. We were both being very stubborn. Finally, we were getting her coat to go home and she said to me: "Go away"! She said it very clearly and with a lot of meaning. Maybe it wasn't such a bad day after all!

December 3
Sue: Sam seems to have entered a new phase of emotional development with much stubbornness, mischievousness, foot stamping, etc. It's difficult, but we are happy to see it. Also, she is making more effort at speech (including "di" for drink).

Robin: Yes, we are seeing this behavior, too. I think we could add persistence to that. If she wants me to chase her, she will come and pull hard on my hand. If I say no, she will keep coming back five or six times.

December 10
Sue: Samantha's coat didn't come home yesterday. Is it at Garfield?

December 11
Sue: Now her coat is home and her shoes are missing!

Robin: Hah! At least Sam always gets home!

Sue: Robin, I love your sense of humor. That was my chuckle for the day!

Christmas Vacation. The kids are all home from school and SBRC has given Alan and me two weeks off from work. We are still in the UCSB Parent Training Class and they suggested that, since Samantha is making great strides, perhaps I should keep a journal during this time. So here it is:

December 19, 1979 - After we left the university this morning, we went out to do
some shopping. Sam fell asleep in the grocery cart and I carried her out to the truck through the rain. I put her head down in my lap and she woke up, sat up, and said "wet".

December 20 - Sam hung around the kitchen, underfoot, while I baked Christmas cookies today. She kept running off with my aluminum measuring spoons that are fastened together. I'm thinking of getting her a set of her own.

December 21 – Sammie is bored today. She keeps asking to go outdoors in the backyard, but it is still raining. Last night Alan tucked her into bed. She always sleeps with a blanket over her head. She had already pulled it over her head when he said, "Hey, what about my kiss?" She threw off the blanket, raised up in bed, and gave him a kiss, all in one motion. Then she rearranged her blanket and went right off to sleep.

December 25 – Christmas Day. Sammie has been awake since 5 a.m. We opened gifts before 7 a.m. Sammie giggled a lot and tore paper off her packages and then showed interest in the contents (new behavior for her). Her two favorite things were small, soft rubber squeaky toys – a porcupine and a lion.

December 26 – We have had a lot of company. Twelve of us for Christmas dinner yesterday (family and friends). Then my brother, his girlfriend, and three of her relatives today. Sammie has been surprisingly receptive – a far cry from the child who used to hide in her bedroom!

December 27 – Quiet day finally! Sammie and Andrea both fell asleep mid-afternoon. Rainy day, fireplace going.

December 28 – Sammie is like a caged tiger today. Too many days indoors without enough structured activity. We are all involved in household activities. Mark and Alan are building a toy box; my 24 year old daughter, Laura, is baking cookies; I am trying to get laundry done; Andrea has a neighbor/friend in to play.

<u>December 29</u> – We had a small gathering of friends this evening for drinks and hors d'oeuvres. Bill and Jeannie Harner, new friends from Alan's gun club, were first to arrive. Just before they entered the house, Samantha had dumped a box of dry spaghetti on the kitchen floor. Jeannie says she will never forget the sight of Samantha and me down on the floor picking up spaghetti like jack-straws!

From that evening forward the Harners were special friends and strong Sammie advocates. Whenever they visited, Sammie gave them big hugs and kisses and then took Jeannie by the hand to go sit with her on her swing, or in her room. When we went out to eat at a restaurant, they always insisted that Sammie accompany us and woe be to anyone who ever criticized or ignored Samantha!

<u>December 31</u> – During vacation Sam has been making growling sounds. We all express our irritation by saying, "Bad sounds, Sammie". Now since working off some of her energy and frustration outdoors, she's switched to syllables like "da, ba, ga". We have been telling her what good sounds they are.

<u>January 3, 1980</u> – First day back at school. No notes from Garfield so I don't know how her day was. When I arrived at Kids N Things, Samantha was in the group in the TV room with Marnie, sitting quietly and apparently watching TV. She is still using her syllables tonight. She said, "Mama, mama, mama" while she was underfoot when I was preparing dinner.

CHAPTER SEVENTEEN

El Rancho School (Sammie's third school transfer)

<u>1980</u> – Garfield School was closed and Samantha was transferred to El Rancho School in Goleta. This is her third school and I was <u>very</u> unhappy about it. Autistic children do not handle changes well at all.

<u>September 10, 1980</u>
New Teacher: Lynne: Samantha had a rough day. Lots of tantrums, very unhappy. She didn't want to be touched at all. She seemed tired, but wouldn't take a nap.

Sue: She hates any change in her environment or routine. It will take her awhile to get used to the new school.

<u>October 1, 1980</u> Samantha's Journal
Lynne: Samantha was hyper today. It was hard for her to get back into the swing of things. We saw some self-help improvements that you must have been working on at home. Such as the way she uses her index fingers to work the back of her shoe on her heel.

Sue: This past week has been a strain for Sam as you can see from the scratches on her face and body.

<u>October 7, 1980</u>
Sue: Samantha was stung by a bee yesterday afternoon and we took her to the hospital in severe allergic reaction. Therefore, she is highly

"sensitized" at the moment and if she should happen to run into another bee, please call the paramedics and get her to the hospital <u>fast</u> ! Use this journal as my written permission for emergency treatment.

<u>Lynne</u> : We were very sorry to hear about Sam's reaction. Would you describe the symptoms involved to help us identify what has happened if we don't actually see she was stung? Her hand didn't seem to bother too much today except for a little scratching. She sure was hyper, though, and cranky. We made a copy of your note for the nurse, Donna Mickelson.

October 8
Sue: Since I, too, have severe allergic reactions to bee stings, I can easily describe the symptoms. When Sammie gets stung, she will indicate by crying and will usually be rubbing the painful spot. This is usually followed by severe localized redness and swelling. Then, in severe reaction, as soon as the venom enters the bloodstream, she would break out in a bright red rash all over her body. This itches so terribly it is indescribable. The rash is followed by puffy swelling of lips, tongue (sometimes eyelids) and that is when it becomes very dangerous because that swelling can be severe enough to suffocate the person.

Lynne: Thanks for the description. I'm sure if it ever happens here, what you've told us will be a big help.

At snack time today we had bananas. Sam had some and then I heard a very distinct "more". Later at lunch she surprised me with "more" and then said it two or three more times. She said it so clearly and distinctly.

October 9
Sue: I have an appointment with Sam's doctor to discuss the best emergency protection for Sammie.

(The doctor prescribed a bee-sting kit containing a hypodermic needle filled with antihistamine)

October 10
Sue: Sam has an appointment on Tuesday with an allergist in downtown Santa Barbara. They claim there is a new desensitization process that will protect her from bee stings.

<u>October 14</u>
Sue: Our trip to the allergist yesterday was a great disappointment for me. Their desensitization would involve a 9-week series of shots (about 15 in all) and then one a month for the rest of her life. I can't put her through that much trauma, so we will have to take our chances with the sting-kits. I have a prescription for 3 of them and plan to buy them today. Yours will be sent to you tomorrow. Please tell Donna Mickelson because she plans to go over the sting-kit directions with you, too.

Lynne: Kit received. Donna gave us all a demonstration so we know we are prepared.

I was quite upset when Samantha was first transferred to El Rancho School and in addition to the fact that change itself is difficult for Samantha, her new teacher (Lynne) was trained to teach mentally retarded children and had no experience in dealing with an autistic child. Finally, after observing Samantha's regression, I appealed to Glenn at UCSB for help. I am going to transcribe directly from Sam's journal for the 1980 school year and you will be able to see the improvements that followed his intervention.

<u>October 15, 1980</u>
Lynne: Samantha pays attention to her lessons for very short periods of time. She does point to herself for "Show me Samantha". She helped to dress a dolly. Does Samantha brush her own hair at home?

<u>October 16</u>
Sue: Samantha makes an effort to comb or brush her hair, but she is not patient enough to do it well. She is doing more talking at home – "Daddy" "done" "bye", etc.

<u>October 16</u>
Lynne: I have not heard "Daddy" and "done" at school, but I have heard "bye". She cooperated in brushing her hair. She is learning the signs for her family members.

<u>October 17</u>
Sue: Please always require an attempt at speech along with the signing. She can, in most cases, at least produce the first syllable.

October 17
Lynne: Samantha paid attention to some of her lessons, but was very distracted during others.

October 20
Sue: Sammie is digging her fingernails into herself again – a self-punishment that had entirely disappeared.

October 20
Lynne: For the first part of the morning Samantha was very responsive. Suddenly she became very frustrated, crying and all sorts of behaviors that prevented her lessons.

October 21
Sue: Sammie arrived home in the same mood described above.

October 21
Lynne: Samantha's mood was better today. She attended to some of her lessons. Thank you very much for the signing book.

October 21
Cheryl: Sammy had a much better day today. She was more communicative, said "water" very clearly and signed often. She was very happy today and very responsive. She's getting so much better in groups! I don't have to lead her lately – she just follows the other kids and sits down where they are. She's listening to the other kids more now when they ask her something or say "hi" to her and she listens well to all the leaders now instead of just to me (on good days).

Samantha was now too old to go to Kids N Things because it was a nursery school. I enrolled her in an after-school program at Mc Kenzie Park and Kathy H. arranged for a one-to-one aid for her. Cheryl is a student at USCB and knew Sammie from the Autism Project.

October 27
Lynne: Samantha seemed more calm and relaxed today than she has been.

<u>October 27</u>
Sue: It always takes Sammie longer to adjust to time changes. She has been awake since 4 a.m.

<u>October 28</u>
Lynne: Samantha had an ok day. Part of the time she was on task and part off task. I hope the men who visited yesterday will soon be able to get back to you to discuss what's next as to what can best help Samantha.
    (Lynne was referring to Glen D. and Rob O'N. from UCSB)

<u>Letter from Glen dated October 29</u>:

Dear Sue:

On Monday, October 28, Rob O'Neill and I observed Sammie in her classroom at El Rancho School. We observed her in her class activities between 9:00 a.m. and 11:15. We also had opportunities to briefly discuss Sammie's curriculum with her teacher, Lynne, her speech therapist and several teacher aides. As per your request, I have compiled a brief summery report of our observations.

1. Sammie's teacher, Lynne seems not only dedicated and very interested in Sammie's welfare, but also quite capable of effective teaching. Her teaching interactions with Sammie (and those of the speech therapist) were positive and generally successful.

2. While the teacher aides were clearly motivated, their teaching methods were not always consistent with those of the teacher. This may cause problems in the way Sammie learns to respond to instructions and to people in general. Sammie would probably benefit from greater consistency in the way that instructions are delivered and in the way off-task behaviors are consequated. As the head teacher seemed to have success with Sammie, we might recommend that her approach be adopted by

everybody who works with Sammie. For example, when Sammie tantrums, the technique of continuing to present instructions until the tantrum subsides is apparently the most successful approach and should be followed by all staff.

3. Sammie would benefit most from having additional school time devoted to structured, directed teaching. While some children may benefit a great deal from unstructured playground time, this does not seem to be the case with Sammie. Since Sammie is not the only child who would benefit from a more formal academic approach, additional structured teaching should meet the needs of all the children in this class.

4. Sammie's learning would probably be accelerated if teaching was focused on a few functional objectives. As Sammie's teacher pointed out, it would be useful to set clear priorities. We would recommend a focus on behaviors which would be of obvious utility for Sammie now and in the future. Such functional objectives would include communication and domestic living skills, (as opposed to puzzles, etc.)

In general, Sammie's current placement at El Rancho has the potential to offer excellent opportunities for learning. If the teaching personnel could consistently use effective teaching methods and if the curriculum was a bit more intensive and functional, this would probably be the best classroom available for Sammie at the present time.

I hope these comments are helpful. Please let us know if we can be of further assistance.

Sincerely,
Glen D.
Research Assistant
UCSB Autism Project

P.S. I am enclosing a few reprints which summarize some useful educational procedures for children such as Sammie. It may be of value to you and the teaching personnel who work with her.
Cc: Lynne

November 4
Sue: Samantha is still in a period of regression as exemplified by her tantrums and her bloody face. We are seeing behavior we haven't seen in 2 years. All I can suggest at the moment is just hang in there and keep on trying to get her cooperation. Work through her tantrums.

Lynne: We are trying to hang in to get Samantha's cooperation and work through her tantrums. We are making an effort to become more consistent with her. Glen has sent us some information that all of us here at school will read. Samantha has to work with so many different people this year! A new aid started with our program yesterday. Samantha had a day in which her behavior and attention were up and down.

Cheryl: Sammie was much happier today. We are hanging in there, too, and working on the cooperation. Lynne, we need to work on the consistency together. If we are not consistent, we will work against each other.

November 6
Sue: Sam's behavior here at home is improving. Maybe she is starting to come back!

Lynne: Sam's behavior improved at school today, too.

November 7
Sue: I hope she continues on the right track for awhile!

Lynne: She was on and off today, but it was a pretty good day

Cheryl: Sammie was even better today than she was yesterday! She seems to be listening better and she is responding after I say something just once. She has been much quieter this week; not many noises, no tantrums, very little crying. She has been pretty happy all week long.

November 17
Alan: Samantha had a good weekend with a long ride to Knotts Berry Farm on Saturday and a quiet day Sunday. Sue is sick today.

Lynne: Sounds like Samantha had a fun weekend. She had a good day at school.

Cheryl: Sammie wasn't listening very well today, but she was happy.

November 18
Lynne: I am very pleased with how Samantha worked today! She was very responsive.

Sue: I am so glad to hear she is beginning to work with you!

November 19
Lynne: Samantha had another very responsive day. She also responded well to the speech therapist.

Cheryl: Samantha has been very responsive and quiet for the past two days. She's been great!

November 20
Sue: Sam is improving in behavior at home, too, and trying to communicate again. Her hair care is more coordinated, but she still tends to comb or brush one place instead of all over.

Lynne: Sam's hair care at school is the same as you describe.

November 26
Lynne: We are working on the numbers 1, 2, 3 and the colors red, blue, yellow and green. We colored a circle and drew a square.

Sue: I'm glad to see you trying to get Sam to draw circles and squares.

She is obviously not showing much interest yet, but don't give up! Have you tried showing her how to manipulate scissors?

Cheryl: When you say Samantha is doing circles and squares, do you mean you are teaching her to draw them? Also, I started her with scissors and she has no problem holding them but she doesn't get the angle correctly. Does Samantha use a fork consistently at home? She has tried to get away with using her hands, but now she knows I won't let her and she's pretty good at using her fork all the time. She was sweetheart today – happy, no tantrums or crying. She was very attentive during crafts and concentrated on what she was doing. I'm working on chaining words with her, especially during snacks. It may take her 15 minutes to say a word to me, but she doesn't get what she wants until she says the first vowel or consonant. What words does she use when she asks for things with you? I use "water" and "drink". I have heard her say "no" and "more" often.

In a phone call from Glen, he said that we should consider adding running to Sam's therapy, especially in the morning before school. They were having some good results with some clients in the autism project and thought Samantha might also benefit.

December 5
Sue: Sammie and I ran from 6 to 6 :20 this morning. I finally talked myself into it. Let me know if you see any good effects because I need encouragement to keep it up.

Lynne: I am glad to know you ran with Samantha this morning! She had a good day at school. She is learning to snap her pants. I am placing my hands over hers and pushing, telling her "push the snap". She can usually pull the zipper up.

Janet (a new aide at McKenzie After-school program): It is wonderful that you are running with Sammie. She is doing great today. She responded very well when playing ball and even said "ball" clearly. She made good attempts to talk today. She responded to "Sammie come" consistently. We are teaching her the sign for want and she is doing very well. She is also giving us good eye contact. Keep up the good work with the running. I think it will make a difference.

December 8

Sue: We are still running every day and Saturday Samantha had a horse-back riding lesson. She loved it!

(A couple of girls from UCSB started a horseback riding therapy project for handicapped children. We enrolled Samantha and she did very well.)

Sam's horseback riding lesson

Horseback riding lesson

Horseback riding lesson

December 10
Sue: Sammie did not get to run this morning because I didn't feel up to it. I sewed a loop in the back of Sammie's coat so it will be easier to hang up. Her coat is slippery.

Lynne: The mornings that Sammie does not run at home, she runs after she gets to school. She was very attentive today.

December 12
Alan: Sue had to return to Michigan for a week or so. You will be dealing with me and, if you need to you can reach me at work. Sammie ran for only a short time and then started crying so her brother brought her back.

Lynne: Samantha had a fine day at school. She practiced writing and cutting, and signing parts of clothes.

Saturday, 13 December, 1980: Alan started a journal page of his own to describe his day!

7:20 am – awoke to a quiet house
1. Found Sammie and Andrea sleeping in the livingroom
2. Went to get dressed and washed contact lenses down drain
3. Put in spares and then cleaned up Sam (she had thrown up in the night)
4. Retrieved lenses from drain trap. Trap leaks.
5. Started breakfast; let son Frank take over – cleaned Sam's bed and did three loads of laundry. Washer does not pump water out!
6. Sears will come out Monday

9:30
7. Sammie throws up again in livingroom sitting by back door

11 am
8. Horseback riding lesson for Sam
9. Went shopping for food
10. Visited Bob Stagat to talk (and joke) about above
11. Arrive home -- Frank outside looking for Sam – she's been gone for

maybe a half hour. Mark, Frank, Andrea and other neighborhood kids are searching neighborhood.

<u>4:00 pm</u>
Went home to call sheriff. Found call waiting from Barbara Walker (former worker with Sammie). Sammie had been found in the middle of a busy street by two young men. They were familiar with autism and knew she was in danger so they picked her up and took her to Devereau School (a residential school for severely handicapped children).

I was greeted with the above story when I arrived at the airport in Santa Barbara upon my return from Michigan!

CHAPTER EIGHTEEN
Improved Reports

<u>January 5, 1981</u>
<u>Sue</u> : Happy New Year! Sammie had a restful vacation. We ran again this morning and we are back on schedule. The only excitement was the day Samantha wandered away from home (which ended well for all concerned) and then a few days ago we took a trip to Goleta Valley Hospital to have a tick removed from her shoulder.

<u>Lynne:</u> Samantha responded very well to all we asked her to do at school today.

<u>January 6</u>
<u>Sue</u> : Sammie ran very willingly and very fast this morning. She's feeling good!

<u>Lynne</u> : Samantha skated during two recesses. She skated almost continually, seldom stopping. She also attempted to play with a ball and a hula hoop. She seemed to enjoy painting with a brush on paper today. She cooperated with what we asked her to do. It appears that your early morning running is making Samantha more responsive during school.

<u>Cheryl</u> : Samantha must have had a busy day. At McKenzie she was very tired and kept falling asleep. Janet and I and the other kids are trying to help Samantha understand the game of tag. She has seemed more willing to play with other children and enjoying them more than before. Your morning running seems to be helping!

January 7
Sue: Sammie definitely appears to be on an upswing. We should see some new development soon.

Lynne : Samantha was very active today. With this beautiful weather she would rather play than do her lessons. Nevertheless, I got her to focus her attention on me during the lessons. Her lessons today were pointing to the family members and signing their names and touching the body parts on a baby doll. Samantha seems to like all the students in this class. She enters the sandbox and plays with all the students around her. Sometimes we play sort of a wrestling game which is simply a big pile-up of children with everyone wriggling on top of each other. Many activities she does right beside other students. Today she kissed Scott on the face and Scott kissed Samantha on the face. I told her to and was surprised when she did so.

January 8
Sue : Thanks for the detailed account of Sam's day. I appreciate it!

Lynne : One lesson Samantha did today was signing and naming apple, orange, pear, and banana.

January 9
Lynne : Samantha's attitude seems to be getting happier and happier. She is cooperating more day by day. Today she had a lesson naming clothes. She also played a little bit with miniature furniture and people.

January 13
Sue : We changed Sam's bedroom around on the weekend. She now has a room of her own. She used to share with Andrea. Possibly because of the change, she's having a lot of night-wakefulness, so don't be surprised if she gets sleepy during the day.

Lynne : Samantha had a good day and she stayed awake.

Cheryl : Samantha was sleepy, but very responsive and attentive. We went to the beach and park. We traced each other's bodies; Samantha told me where her different body parts were and we did some tactile exercises. Samantha has been more tolerant of affection from other children lately.

January 15
Sue : Alan measured the distance Sammie and I run and it turned out to be 1/2 mile per day! We are about to increase the distance.

January 21
Sue : I'm so glad her journal was found! I've saved her notebooks since she was 2 years old and they are a very important record of her development. Thanks!

Lynne: Samantha learned the signs for popcorn and crackers today.

Cheryl : Sammie played tag with me today! She's getting the hang of it little by little. She kicked a ball around the field while running for about 7 minutes. When we stopped playing and I let her have free time, she looked at me and said "Want play" and ran after tagging me. This is the first time she has spontaneously chained two words together. I was so happy!

January 29
Sue : This is the first day in January that Sammie and I have not run. Too much rain this morning.

February 3
Sue : Sammie is using more language and signs again – very encouraging!

Lynne : Samantha signs at school to try to get what she wants. She doesn't always use correct signs, but uses the old signs that she knew before over and over. But she is definitely making lots of attempts to communicate with us. Everyone here in the classroom have become her friends. She will hug each person.

February 4
Sue : We had a cold run this morning. Very invigorating! Sammie has started a new thing that needs to be discouraged. She is putting her head

on her arm or on the table when she eats. If she is trying it at school, please don't allow it.

Lynne : Samantha has been eating better all the time at school. She likes to play with us at recess.

February 9
Sue : It wasn't raining at 6 am so we had a good run.

Janet : Cheryl is sick today so it's Janet and Sammie. She listened to me the whole time she was here and I didn't have to raise my voice once!

February 17
Sue : Sam went ice skating and got a huge blister on her toe on her right foot. It's sore enough that she can't wear shoes and is willing to wear a band-aid on it.

February 18
Alan : Sam's toe is still tender, but as you can see, she will put shoes on.

Lynne : Does Samantha ice skate as well as she roller skates?

Cheryl : Yes, Sammie skates on ice almost as well as she roller skates. All she needs is practice. She really concentrates when she's on ice. She didn't fall once, the little munchkin!

February 19
Sue : It's wonderful that Sammie is learning to do more things. You would enjoy watching her horseback riding lessons. She cantered for the first time Saturday and kept her balance beautifully. At home she is more and more interested in toys and things. As she fills her time with more "normal", acceptable activities, maybe more of her autistic behaviors will recede.

Lynne : Samantha is starting to get the idea of opening and closing scissors for the purpose of cutting. She is showing some interest in scribbling with pretty colored markers.

<u>Cheryl</u> : When we go out to the playground, Sammie now shows more interest in the equipment. In October, she would only spin the merry-go-round and watch it. Now she gets on the merry-go-round and pushes herself on it. She goes to the slide before I even ask her to and will play by herself on it. She climbs on the jungle gym, too. She's showing more interest in playing ball with others. She'll kick it back and forth now, watch where it's going (usually) and throw it back.

<u>Sue</u>: Great news from both sources! Thanks for writing. Sam's toe is better and I'll send her skates on Monday.

<u>February 23</u>
<u>Sue</u> : Sammie and I ran again today.

<u>Lynne</u> : Samantha is using colored markers on paper and today she did a big picture, concentrating on it for at least 10 minutes.

<u>Cheryl</u> : We took Samantha to play tennis with the younger children. She was much more tolerant and willing to learn than last time. She kept her eye on the ball and hit one herself. Her attention to task has been tremendous lately. She seems to be appreciative of challenging tasks rather than being frustrated as before.

All of Samantha's journal reports continued to show improvements in all areas. She was becoming an active, happy, cooperative child.

At the end of March we (Alan, Sammie, Andrea, and I) took a weekend trip to the San Diego Zoo. We had a wonderful time. Sammie's behavior was remarkably appropriate. She enjoyed the tour bus, looked at all the animals, loved the bird sanctuary, rode on the moving stairway with no fear, walked for miles, and ate peanuts and ice cream cones. In the evening, we had dinner at Kelly's Steak House, a very nice restaurant adjacent to the motel that we stayed in and, again, Sammie's behavior was perfect. Back at the motel, she enjoyed an after-dark dip in a nice, warm Jacuzzi. That was the nicest family outing we had ever had!

<u>April 21, 1981</u> Today is Samantha's 10th birthday. Alan's parents came down from San Francisco to join in the celebration. Sammie successfully blew out all the candles on her birthday cake. Later, each time her

grandpa lit his pipe, she blew out the match. This is the first time that I haven't felt like crying on her birthday. She and I are both making progress!

By the beginning of May, Sam and I were running a full mile at 6 in the morning before she went to school. One morning when I got up I found Sam in the livingroom with her pajamas off. She was trying to get her running suit on! I took that to mean that she enjoys her runs.

Samantha is doing her home tasks without prompting. When she finishes her meals, she carries her dishes to the sink and washes her hands. When I say "It's bath time", she pops into the bathroom, goes potty, and removes her clothes.

By the end of May, she was dressing herself with only supervision and coaching on my part.

In September, lack of school funding raised its ugly head again, as noted in the following letters.

September 9, 1981
Letter from Lynne (Sam's teacher) to Steve (Director, Pupil Personnel/Special Services)

"I am extremely concerned about the possible lack of student safety for my students during the 1981-1982 school year. I am especially concerned for the safety of Samantha Brown. In the past she has evaded the watchful attention of trained personnel and has left the school grounds. This year the trained personnel assigned to my program has been cut.

The personnel must divide their attention equally among the 15 students in the combined SH/LH program, but Samantha takes a full time attention. The danger of Samantha evading supervision and leaving the school grounds is most extreme during the recess times at 10:15-10:30 and 12:00-12:15. Although I (and the rest of the staff) will do our utmost to ensure the proper supervision of Samantha and the rest of our students, I am asking to be relieved of liability for Samantha's safety during the times indicated above. We do not have enough personnel to ensure Samantha's safety."

<u>September 22, 1981</u>
I received a copy of another letter concerning Samantha's safety (or lack thereof) without a one-to-one aide:

> To Kathy H., Tri-Counties Regional Center from the Recreation Supervisor of Develcamp (a summer program Samantha attended after school)

> "Dear Kathy: This past summer one of your clients, Samantha Brown, attended our Develcamp Program. I felt that a report from us would be helpful in her future recreational and camp programming.

> The camp and recreational setting seems to be beneficial for Sam. She enjoys the activities, friends, and openness of the program. While a little reluctant, she will enter the pool and seems to enjoy herself. Several of our recreation leaders have a special friendship with Sam. They see her on a daily basis after school hours.

> We do, however, have a problem with supervision for Sam. Our camp is geared for a three-to-one overall participant/staff ratio. The older, more capable participants function on even less staff/participant ratio. Sam cannot function on this level. She has no sense of danger, runs away from groups, and has difficulty with compliance. We constantly modify activities and work on behavioral goals for the participants in order to better serve their needs. Our camp, however, is not geared for the one-to-one situation that Sam needs. We found that the only way to keep her safe from danger was to hold her hand from 9:00 am when she arrived at camp until 4:00 pm when she left. This tied up our recreation leader and prevented her from working with the group.

In the future, we will only accept Sam in our recreational and camp program if she is accompanied by an aide. While I think these programs are beneficial for Samantha, I don't feel we can offer the supervision she needs."

September 24, 1981
Letter from me to Steve:

"In view of the concern expressed to you in Lynne's letter regarding playground safety and the Develcamp Supervisor's letter regarding her concerns regarding Samantha's safety, I am hereby requesting a full review of her educational program and her present placement. It is abundantly clear that Samantha needs one-to-one supervision.

In addition to the representative from your department, I would like representatives from the Evaluation Assessment Service Center and Tri-Counties Regional Center to attend. Please let me know a date and time that is suitable as soon as possible."

CHAPTER NINETEEN:

Trying to get a one-to-one aide

At about this point in time, Alan traded his Carryall for a 7-passenger Chevrolet Leisure van. Whenever Samantha was not in school, we took some wonderful van-camping trips. Sammie loved traveling in the van and she and Andrea always had a good time on the road.

September 26, 1981

Kathy H. sent me some information from Gary Hart, Assemblyman, California Legislature, regarding Block Grants and asked me to prepare a request for after school care funding. I prepared the following:

OBJECTIVE: PROVIDE AFTER-SCHOOL
CARE FOR HANDICAPPED CHILDREN

INTRODUCTION: Working parents of handicapped children have fewer options for suitable after-school care than parents of "normal" children. Most normal children are provided with after-school programs (i.e., Gazebo Learning Center, After School Project, Girls Club, etc.). Most of these groups will not accept handicapped children into their programs. If a parent does not opt for public programs, there is always neighborhood care available for the normal child. Neighbors (private care people) also will not accept handicapped children. Working parents of handicapped children need a child-care program geared to the special needs of our special children.

GOALS: With the recent and continuing budget cuts in special education funding, the schools are providing less and less for our children. It is up to the parents and the community at large to supplement the dwindling programs.

Our children, as human beings, need to

+ develop skills that give her/him a sense of competence
+ develop mutually supportive ways of interacting with children and adults
+ gain an understanding and functioning knowledge of the environment and the people in it

All children's intellectual development proceeds through stages. Each stage is built on skills and information obtained in the previous one. The child's cognitive development depends not only on maturation or the central nervous system – the gradual control over reflexes – but also the experiences in her/his environment. Formal instruction and rote learning (as provided by the school system) is not the most important variable. What is important is the richness of stimuli that challenges a child and the opportunities she or he has for manipulating materials at every stage of development. Playing is a child's way to experience, to touch, to feel, to try out, to question, and to <u>learn.</u> Unfortunately, a developmentally disabled child does not self-initiate these kinds of experiences. Our goal, therefore is to provide our children with a day-care center that will give her/him countless opportunities to manipulate real things in a real world. We intend to staff our center with people trained and dedicated toward leading our children to play, discovery and exploration based on the child's age, abilities, and interests.

SPECIFIC ACTIVITIES
Indoor play

<u>Dramatic Play</u> . An area designed to look like a house, containing materials that might stimulate play-acting of familiar roles: parent, baby, teacher, etc. There would be household equipment, tools, dolls, hats, shoes, coats, dresses, telephones and other accessories children see every day.

Water play might be included in this area. Large tubs for the water; various sized containers with different-sized openings. Food coloring and soap flakes could be added.

Children can wash dolls, toys, etc. For further experimentation, straws, funnels, tubes, egg beaters, squeeze bottles could be added.

Food preparation should be included to give the children experiences in helping to prepare snacks or simple meals.

Manipulative Toys and Group Games. This area would provide assorted sizes of plastic balls. Games would be devised to improve eye-hand coordination, e.g. rolling a ball along a line taped to the floor; tossing a ball through an eye-level hoop-ring; indoor baseball with large plastic bats to play "tee-ball", eventually progressing to "slow pitch" baseball; indoor bowling.

Woodworking might be included in this area. A sturdy table with large pieces of soft wood nails, a hammer, and sandpaper.

Music. Drums, shakers, bells, tambourines, horns, as well as phonograph and records.

Library. A rocking chair, rugs, couches, anything comfortable where the children can read or look at and touch books, magazines, pictures.

Outdoor Play
We need a fully-enclosed play yard with the usual swings, slides, and climbing equipment, a sandy area, and a grass area. Additional outdoor activities would eventually include field trips, hikes, bus rides, beach experiences, etc.

Indoor play
Dramatic Play . An area designed to look like a house, containing materials that might stimulate play-acting of familiar roles: parent, baby, teacher, etc. There would

be household equipment, tools, dolls, hats, shoes, coats, dresses, telephones and other accessories children see every day.

Water play might be included in this area. Large tubs for the water; various sized containers with different-sized openings. Food coloring and soap flakes could be added. Children can wash dolls, toys, etc. For further experimentation, straws, funnels, tubes, egg beaters, squeeze bottles could be added.

Food preparation should be included to give the children experiences in helping to prepare snacks or simple meals.

Kathy Hunter made some additions to the above request and we sent it off to Gary Hart. However, I was still in a bind for after school care for Samantha until Janet (her aide at McKenzie Park and special friend) volunteered to care for her. Janet had been working at Develcamp, but we were able to arrange for her to take Samantha back to McKenzie Park's after-school program.

October 7, 1981
Lynne asked me to meet with her and Samantha's speech teacher to show them exactly how I worked on speech with Samantha at home. On the morning that I was preparing to go to school with Sammie for that meeting, Samantha finger-painted the kitchen and her hair with butter. She made some nice designs on the dining room table!

Lynne (Sam's teacher), Kathy H. (Tri-Counties Regional Center), and I have been trying for several months to get in-service training in Sammie's classroom. Lynne is well-trained and very capable in teaching mentally retarded children. Samantha is a whole different story and Lynne is getting frustrated. We are asking the school board to provide training in how to teach an autistic child for Lynne and her aides.

November 19, 1981 Letter from the Director of Pupil Personnel/ Special Services to Dr. Oliver, PhD, Director of Tri-Counties Regional Center:

"I'm sorry I've been unable to get in contact with you recently and thought I would write this letter to ask a question about Samantha Brown. As you know, Samantha was placed in our Severely Handicapped program for trainable mentally retarded about a year and a half ago and I've been working with Mrs. Brown and the classroom teacher, Lynne, in attempting to meet Samantha's many needs.

One of the recent developments has been a need for some in-service training on behavioral techniques in working with Samantha. I have been in contact with Glen D. from the autistic project at UCSB and he has indicated that he would be willing to provide in-service to Lynne, specifically, and the aides, in how better to manage some of the behavioral manifestations in the classroom. Mrs. Brown also feels strongly that this is needed.

My question is whether TCRC, as part of the services you offer, would be able to cover the costs of these behavioral in-services for our classroom teacher and aides. In my last discussion with Glen and Lynne, they have indicated a need for fifteen (15) hours at $16.00 per hour.

I would appreciate a call from you as soon as possible. We do feel an urgent need for this in the management of Samantha at school. Thank you for your attention to this."

January 27, 1982 Letter from me to the Director, Pupil Personnel/ Special Services:

"This is to appeal once again for in-service on behavioral management with Lynne's staff as offered by Glen D. of UCSB. Your suggestion that I contact Dr. Oliver at TCRC is not acceptable.

Your inaction may have saved your budget, but Samantha and Lynne are the losers.

Samantha is highly agitated within the classroom. She has reverted to hand-biting and stabbing herself with her fingernails – symptoms that point directly to the help that is needed and is available from Glen D's university group. The people at the university have had 2-1/2 years of clinical experience with Samantha."

February 22, 1982 Letter from Dr. Oliver to the Director, Pupil Personnel/Special Services:

"We have discussed your letter of November 19, 1981 on several occasions, most recently on February 19, 1982. Since the issue seems to continue to arise regarding your question, I decided it would be necessary to formally respond to your letter.

Tri-Counties Regional Center cannot purchase the services of Glen D. for the purpose of providing in-service training in behavioral technology to your instructor, Lynne. The reasons are that Mr. D. represents a generic agency, that he is not licensed, and that TCRC can provide equivalent service at much less than the requested rate of $16.00 per hour."

Comment from me after receiving this news: I am not happy about the in-service proposal change! I keep complaining because the knowledge and the methods employed in clinic at UCSB don't filter out to the community. Now I see why! The community is too short sighted and too conscious of purse strings.

February 26, 1982 Letter to Mrs. English, President of Goleta School Board from the Executive Director of the Association for Retarded Citizens:

"It is our understanding that the Goleta School Board has

decided, for reasons unknown, to discontinue classes for the severely handicapped in the Goleta School District.

This decision to close said classes is in itself an unfortunate one; however, our primary concern is with the process through which the parents of the children attending these classes were notified regarding this pending closure. The parents were requested to attend a meeting on 22 February 1982 to allegedly discuss the future programming of their children. At this meeting, casual remarks were made regarding the transfer of children to the Santa Barbara School District. When questions were raised by the parents regarding more specificity as to where the children would be placed, the type of classes, as well as under whose tutelage their children would, they received evasive responses by the staff attending the meeting.

Two days later on 24 February, your Board held a meeting in order to discuss various issues, one of which was the closure of the classes for the severely handicapped. However, this item appeared on the agenda as "Reclassification of Certified Employees." One must question why such vague labeling was employed and why parents whose children are attending the classes for the severely handicapped were not apprised of the fact that they could provide input or voice their objections to the anticipated change.

It seems that the parents are always the victims of decisions made on the administrative level without being given sufficient time or the opportunity to provide their input and make their wishes known.

Our organization, which represents the parents of handicapped children, feels that you and your Board must be made aware of the lack of courtesy extended to the parents in not providing them with the whole picture or the ramifications thereof, not to mention the vagueness as to what might be expected by the parents for their children in the new classes.

It is our intention to watch these developments closely and see to it that the parents receive timely notification in order that they be provided with the opportunity to participate in the decision-making process with regard to the well-being of their children, as outlined in the various laws pertaining to the educational system."

Copies of the above letter were sent to me and to 3 other parents, the Assistant Superintendent of Special Education at Santa Barbara Schools, our Assemblyman, the Executive Director of Area IX Board, ARC-SBC Board of Directors, and Goleta Union School District Board of Trustees.

March 3, 1982 : My letter to the Special Education Administrator (former title Director, Pupil Personnel/Special Services):

"It is time for Samantha Brown's annual review and time for the Independent Education Program to be written. Due to the possible disruption and confusion later on in this year in conjunction with the closing of the entire classroom, I want this done now to ensure a smooth transition and a clearly defined program for Samantha for the coming year. The date I would suggest is March 17 at 3 p.m. I will want Kathy H. in attendance in addition to your staff."

March 4, 1982 : Samantha's Annual Review prepared by Kathy H.:

"Samantha Jo Brown, now almost 11 years old, is a tall slender young girl with blond hair, blue eyes and a fair complexion. Developmentally disabled in association with postnatal viral encephalitis, Samantha has autistic-like behaviors, and limited speech. Samantha continues to attend the Severely Handicapped class at El Rancho

School. It is anticipated that she will attend a new school in September since the students in the handicapped classes at El Rancho School are all being switched to alternative school placements and these classes are being discontinued. TCRC funds an aide to work with Samantha after school due to her need for one on one attention.

Samantha continues to be a more sociable child. She seems to be more aware of her environment and looks for interaction (hugs). She continues to need to acquire age-appropriate social and play skills. Without ongoing supervision and direction, Samantha quickly slips into activities of a self-stimulatory nature. She needs continued exposure to a language environment. Structured after-school programming and summer/vacation programming continues to be a need.

Samantha continues to need a program focused on the acquisition of language. She is scheduled to begin assessment and therapy at UCSB Speech and Language in March at the beginning of the new quarter. A report of their evaluation will be requested when completed. Samantha is scheduled for a review of her educational programming, at mother's request, on 3/17/82."

March 4, 1982:

To: UCSB Speech and Hearing Center
From: Kate B. Speech/Language Specialist, El Rancho School
Re: Samantha Brown

Mrs. Brown has requested that I write to you regarding Samantha Brown's speech program at El Rancho School.

At a review meeting 10-1-81 and parent conference 10-13-81, it was decided that my work with Samantha this school year would emphasize speech only rather than oral/manual as had been the case in prior years with other clinicians. This was decided on because of (1) Samantha's slow progress in sign language and (2) parental desire to establish oral communication. Currently at school Samantha uses the following signs spontaneously: play, music, potty, and please. These are used in limited situations with some non-traditional signs. She attempts to imitate a variety of others.

Samantha's strategy when presented with verbal imitation tasks in October 1981 appeared to be to randomly respond with the various sounds in her repertoire until she happened on the right one and was reinforced. We therefore began by trying to establish consistent imitation of sounds she already used in her spontaneous vocalization (pa and wa). She was reinforced with bites of banana and verbal praise for correct responses.

Samantha learned quickly when only one sound was required, but her rate of progress slowed when she was required to discriminate between two in her imitative attempts. Currently we are maintaining (pa and wa) on intermittent reinforcement and attempting to introduce another sound (ah). Samantha has used (pa and wa) in a game-like sense; On the way to the speech room she has several times grabbed my face and turned it toward her and said (pa or wa) which I would imitate.

Samantha has been unable to consistently imitate oral movements or positions, or sounds. She does not maintain steady phonation during vocalization. When observed blowing into a recorder in her class, she did not make lip closure. Chewing and feeding have presented problems. When attempts are made to manipulate the oral structures manually to evoke a sound, the muscles appear to be held rigidly.

My specific questions/concerns include: (1) The optimum communication mode for Samantha; (2) Pre-speech language skills that should be developed; (3) Pre-speech motor or sensory skills that may be needed.

I am interested in working with you in whatever approach or format would best benefit Samantha and specifically would appreciate any observations related to the above questions/concerns.

Sincerely, Kate B. MA,CCC

March 11, 1982

Letter from me to the President of Goleta Union School Board:

"Since you publicly chastised me last evening for bringing an issue into a public meeting that should have been brought out in a "closed session", please let me apologize for my ignorance of the political nuances involved. And, also, please allow me to hereby repeat my comments – and please feel free to use them in one of your "closed sessions", as you see fit.

When the economic factors were more favorable to Special Education than they are now, the Director of Special Education tried to recruit my daughter Samantha for the Goleta severely handicapped program. I refused because Samantha had a one-to-one aide in her program at Garfield and was progressing nicely and I did not want to upset her balance. When they closed the Garfield program, Samantha was placed in the El Rancho school without my being consulted. Now Samantha is being moved again. She will lose at least six months in trying to orient herself to totally new surroundings. Is it the purpose of this administrator to keep us all confused, upset and off balance?

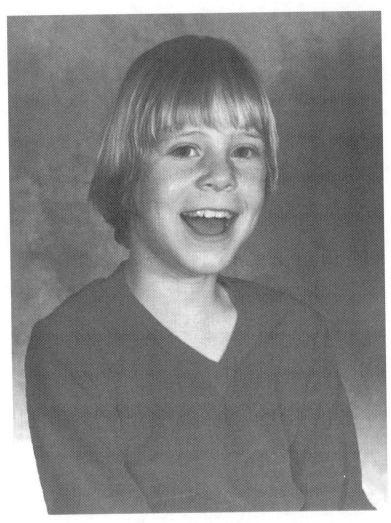

Sammie, Fall 1981

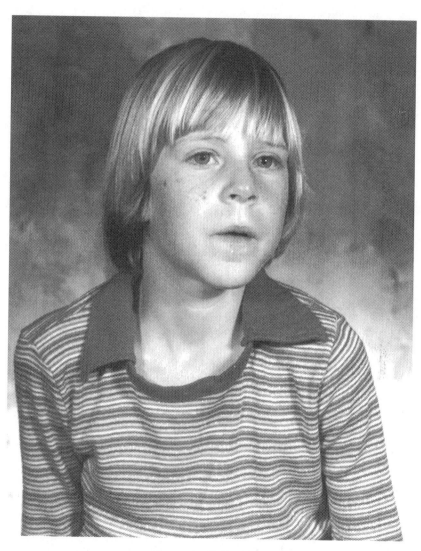

Sammie, Fall 1982

Since Samantha has been at El Rancho school, there has been no one-to-one aide for her (although it has been clearly demonstrated that this is the only way she can learn); an aide was cut from the existing program, and the remaining aide's time was cut to 5-1/4 hours. It took until last month to get one full time aide in this classroom. When the bus arrives at school, the children are met by two teachers (with no aide) to not only keep Sam safe, but keep track of and potty the rest of the children.

Lynne is an outstanding teacher for Samantha. She has not been supported by the district. There is in-service training on teaching autistic children that is available to Lynne, her team-mates and the aides. It has taken this administrator from November until now to implement this training, although the money is and has been available.

Complete diagnostic assessment of Samantha's abilities and potential has also been available. No one told me about it until February 24th of this year. I feel this information was deliberately withheld from me for budgetary reasons.

My point is that this outstanding program could have been better administrated. It could still be in existence next year if it had been."

<u>March 17, 1982</u> This is the meeting I requested in my letter to Steve, the Special Education Administrator:

MINUTES OF THE INDEPENDENT EDUCATION PROGRAM FOR SAMANTHA BROWN: PRESENT:

Kathy H, Tri-Counties Regional Center
Kathy B., Speech Therapist, Goleta Union School District
Eileen M, Parent Advocate
Lynne, Severely Handicapped Class Teacher
Aime P., Program Specialist, County School District
Steve, Administrator, Special Education, Goleta School
Bill E., School Psychologist, Goleta School District
John K., Adaptive Physical Education, Goleta School District

I was there, too, but I was neither introduced nor acknowledged.

Steve: We will begin by reviewing the current program and summer school.

Lynne: We will list Goals and Objectives and Achievement in that order.
   Eye Contact: Will follow flashlight path: achieved
   Skating: Will skate in straight line: does not
   Social Ability: Will greet given classmates: does not
   Will give name tag and picture to person: does not
   Will increase in self-care ability: not achieved
   Will wash and dry hands independently: does not
   Will brush top and sides of hair: does only with prompts
   Vestibular Motor Ability: Will appropriately scribble for 5 minutes: Objective achieved
   To increase leisure time skills: Will independently play tape recorder: Objective achieved
   To increase academic skills: squares, circles, rectangles: has not learned "labels"; will match by shape, not by name
   Will go "on" or "under": does not
   Adaptive PE: Distinguish body parts, neck muscles, upper torso: does
   Will throw and catch ball; kick with feet; will increase
   Body awareness: not achieved
   Communication: Will spontaneously sign with spoken word: maintained, has not increased; not spontaneous, only with prompts
   Language and Music activities: has improved in attention and involvement
   Will learn signs and concepts of red light, green light: not achieved
   Introduce refusal sign: not achieved in school

Steve: Does she not know, or is she not attending to task?

Steve: Do you have plans or ideas for new programs? Or will you continue with these?

Lynn: We will start new programs

Kathy H: What are your formal speech objectives?

Kathy B.: When we met in November, signing was not going well. We started working on "nonsense syllables" imitatively. She will do one at a time, but will not combine them.

John K.: Her adaptive PE objectives were written without consultation. My own analysis would probably come up with different needs, such as: (1) Ability to sustain motor planning (she cannot do this), for example, to ride a scooter board from one end of the room to another, as opposed to "open ended" activities; (2) Muscle tone. She is tense, needs relaxation type things.

Steve: Have you been working in this direction?

John: She has "off-task" behaviors, stimming, etc. After working through the behaviors, she still has motor planning difficulties. She needs to be involved in activities where motor skills are incorporated. She has difficulty with bouncing balls, rolling balls, striking balls, kicking a moving ball; she is not consistent in performance. She has needs we cannot meet. I have seen her infrequently on a weekly (and now bi-weekly) basis. Basically, Lynne is carrying out the program. The equipment is carried from school to school throughout the district.

Kathy H.: She needs more PE than a weekly session. The school needs to refer her to California Children's Service.

Steve: She may be ineligible for their service. They usually take children on a "medical need" basis.

John: Is Samantha on medication? She is a difficult child to work with; it's hard to meet goals. One must first break through her barriers, which we don't often do. She needs a behavior technician, she needs consistency in her program.

Sue: (OK, I have been sitting here listening quietly, biting my lips to keep from shouting). I said: "She needs a one-to-one aide!" I got a couple of "looks", but was ignored!

Kathy B: Yes. I need another person with a stopwatch to take data. I also do not know the levels of expectation for autistic children. What criteria is she supposed to meet?

Steve: Neither Lynne, Kathy, John, nor Bill have training for autistic children. John, do you believe these objectives should continue for Sam?

John: They should continue, but they have not been met because of lost time, off-task behavior, etc. Sometimes it appears I am seeing accomplishment of activities and then we are back to Square One. In terms of goals, we need to be realistic. I am not overly optimistic about attaining goals. This is based in part on the fact that I am not here. Secondly, her off-task behavior and stimming makes her inattentive, difficult. I also have to work with the other kids. I spend a relatively short time working with Sam when I am here. Lynne and I have not discussed future plans.

Lynne: She does lie on a mat and get her back rubbed on a daily basis. We also have vigorous activities: running, skating, to release some of her energy. The rest of her program is basic motor skills.

John: She needs relaxation therapy.

Steve: Could she learn to do these?

John: It should be incorporated in her activities. She gets all the things she needs in a general kind of way. We are not dealing in clinical or prescriptive PE. We have no direct service. There are 4 children from Lynne's group, two from the LH class, for approximately 45 minutes on a biweekly basis.

Sue: Samantha needs a one-to-one aide! It has been demonstrated time after time that this is the only way she learns; the only way to keep her on task.

Steve: If that were possible, it would have occurred. We simply do not have the ability. There is no way we can get an additional aide.

Kathy: Would the county provide one-to-one?

Steve: In the county program, the directors and coordinators determine how they will be staffed. Basically, I am powerless. I cannot add aides. The decisions are made by the total county. Anyway, this is not an item for the IEP. Class size, teachers, or how many aides are not issues for the IEP. It will take from 3 to 7 weeks before we have a response from the diagnostic center.

John: Has there ever been a full assessment?

Lynne: A full assessment has never been done. All her records say is: "We tried an assessment and failed."

Steve: Since it could be a while before the diagnostic center can make a decision, let's finish the goals and objectives for now.

The end result of this meeting was that Kathy H. (Sam's caseworker from Tri-Counties Regional Center) got funding for Janet to act as Sam's facilitator after school. Sam's school days ended at 2:00 pm and Janet worked with her until I got home from work at 5 pm. Janet wrote up her own goals and objectives as follows:

<u>March 1982:</u>
PART I: I have begun working with Sammie as her facilitator, but I have been working with her off and on for about three years. I have observed Sammie in school, at home, and at recreation programs, giving me the understanding of how Sammie acts in these different surroundings. Sammie has also started speech therapy at UCSB Autism clinic and so far she is doing very well.

I am working on all of the objectives each day of the week for the consistency that Sammie needs. Sammie rocks, hyperventilates, picks up objects and rubs them together in her hands, bites her hand, pinches herself and other stimming activities. When told to "Stop, Sammie", "no noise", "no hyperventilating", or just plain "Sammie no" she stops her activity most of the time. When this doesn't work or Sam is having a tantrum, I turn away from her until she calms down and then we complete he activity.

PART II: OBJECTIVE 1 – Sensory Motor

<u>Tactile</u>: massage of back, feet, etc., using lotion in massage, different textures, and joint compression. Sammie resists any part of tactile, having

tantrums right away when I ask her to lie down. Several times during tactile, she is also very rigid.

Vestibular:
(+ equals consistent response and – equals inconsistent response)
Nystagnus (spinning) -; Jumping +; Hopping -; Rolling +; Wheelbarrow +; Crab walk -; Knee walking -; Throwing +; Catching +; Running +; Motor Planning +; Protective extension +

Appropriate Play: Sammie would be perfectly content stimming on whatever objects are around for her to rub in her hands, but she does initiate going on the slide, swing, etc., about 10% of the time.

Coloring: For a long time now Sammie has been drawing just lines back and forth. Now Sammie is drawing circles. I noticed when Sammie is not watching what she is doing, her drawing is back and forth lines, but when she is paying attention to what she is doing, she makes nice round circular motions.

Tying shoes: We have started pulling the strings tight, crossing them, putting one under the other and pulling it tight. Samantha has demonstrated the ability to do this with my prompts, but will not pay attention without the prompts.

Group Participation: Sitting with back straight and quietly in group circle; participating in group activities; learning to take turns; walking with the group or person (next to them); holding onto hand when crossing the street.

OBJECTIVE 2: SPEECH (VERBAL)

Sammie can say "Want, Play, Bye, Water, More, Tag". She can connect words such as "Want more". She makes lots of sounds and can repeat a sound that I make when she wants to. Sammie uses signs along with the words and uses a few signs that she does not know the word for. She is relying less and less on signs and is talking a lot more. I am having Sammie talk as much as possible. For example, if she wants to play, she has to say "want play", or if she wants more banana, she has to say "want more b".

OBJECTIVE 3: SWIMMING AND ROLLERSKATING

<u>Swimming</u>: putting self in water; walking in water holding onto side; walking in water without holding onto side; floating with assistance/unassisted; blowing bubbles (closing mouth); kicking feet; moving arms (dog paddling); getting head wet (under water); playing with ball, jumping, etc.

Sammie is very apprehensive in the pool and grabs onto me anytime I get close enough to her (which I am trying to extinguish). I have been using a life-saver ring around her waist which forces her to use her arms to swim to keep afloat. With my constant prompts "kick your feet, Sammie", she gets a few little kicks. She puts her legs apart, but I have been motoring her through the kicking to give her the right idea.

<u>Rollerskating</u>: skating backwards; skating on one foot; skating low, bending her knees; skating over objects; learning how to stop (with stoppers); twirls.

Sammie is a very good skater and I am trying to challenge her by giving her more difficult stunts.

PART THREE: (1) Goals your client has fully achieved; (2) Goals your client has partially achieved; (3) Goals your client has not met or demonstrated significant growth.

I will be working on the three objectives with Sammie for the next quarter from April 1st until June 30th.

End of Report

After hearing all the negativity from the participants in Samantha's IEP, Janet was like a breath of fresh air, an angel in disguise, and Samantha's best friend!

<u>May 19, 1982</u> : I received this letter from the Diagnostic School for Neurologically Handicapped Children;

Dear Parents:

Your child has been referred by your local school district for evaluation at the Diagnostic School. The decision of the Diagnostic School Admissions and Review Committee was to accept your child for evaluation.

The role of the Diagnostic School is to provide evaluation services to local school districts which will result in specific findings and recommendations. These findings and recommendations will assist your district in developing an individualized education program (IEP) and in determining an appropriate classroom placement for your child.

Please be aware that it may be several months before your child is given a specific evaluation date. Written notification will be sent to you three weeks prior to the evaluation date. Your cooperation in completing the necessary forms and returning them to the Diagnostic Center School as soon as possible will expedite the evaluation process.

We look forward to working with you and your child.

Sincerely,
Superintendent

CHAPTER TWENTY

Sammie's 4th New School

<u>June 23, 1982</u> Samantha has been transferred to yet another school. This is her 4th transfer and, ironically, she is back in Hollister, the school she started out in!

<u>Flora, Teacher</u>: Hi, I am looking forward to meeting you. We use these notebooks to communicate daily. Sammie seems to be adjusting well. We are all enjoying working with her.

<u>Sue</u>: I'm glad you use the notebook system! Sam has carried them since she was 2 years old and I have most of them saved. Janet will add to it, too,

<u>June 28, 1982</u>
<u>Sue</u>: Flora, did you know that if you give Sammie something to hold in her hands while you are presenting a task, it cuts down her stims? At home we use a beanbag frog; Mary (Speech therapist at UCSB) used a rag doll.

<u>Flora</u>: No, I didn't know that, but thanks for the information. We have found a few things that calm Sammie. She really likes our net swing, push button musical toy and hand massage vibrator. She is doing well. Janet visited today. We appreciated her input. We talked about Sammie's jogging. I am going to get a copy of the UCSB research article. Janet said you used to do morning jogs. Do you still do that?

June 29. 1982

Sue: No, we haven't run in the morning for awhile. We got a bicycle built for two, but that didn't last long because Sam kept leaning back and forth, almost upsetting us!

September 9, 1982 First day of school

Sue: Sammie's ready and anxious to go. Good luck!

Flora: Sammie had a great day! She seemed happy to be here. Also, I read in her records that she is allergic to bees and needs to have a bee sting kit with her. Do you have one?

September 10, 1982

Sue: Sam's bee sting kit and its instructions are in her backpack. That kit is for the school; it does not need to be sent back and forth.

Janet's Social Facilitation Quarterly Report

NAME OF CLIENT: Samantha Brown
NAME OF FACILITATOR: Janet L.
TIME PERIOD COVERED: July 1, 1982 through September 30, 1982

I.   SPECIFIC OBJECTIVE: Sammie will participate in peer group experience sitting up straight with hands in lap, quietly, for 15 minutes of a 30 minute group session for three consecutive sessions.

II. BASELINE DATA: Sammie participates in peer group experience slouching, making noises, biting her hand, tantruming 25 minutes of a 30 minute session.

III. TECHNIQUES USED TO PROMOTE DESIRED GROWTH: Prompting, praise, modeling.

IV. END OF QUARTER DATA: Sammie participates in peer group experiencing sitting up straight with hands in lap quietly for 15 minutes of a 30 minute group session for three consecutive sessions; therefore, this objective was met.

V.   PROPOSED SPECIFIC OBJECTIVE FOR NEXT QUARTER: Sammie will swim 10 laps moving her arms and legs (with assistance from life preserver) in a 30 minute period.

VI. BASELINE DATA: Sammie swam half laps moving only her arms (with life preserver) in a 30 minute period.

VII. TECHNIQUES USED TO PROMOTE DESIRED GROWTH: Verbal praise and prompting, modeling, and reward (10 minutes in Jacuzzi)

VIII. END OF QUARTER DATA: Sammie swam 20 laps moving her arms and legs (with preserver) in a 30 minute period; therefore, her goal of 10 laps was met.

PROPOSED OBJECTIVES FOR NEXT QUARTER

I.   SPECIFIC OBJECTIVE: Sammie will be more articulate in the words she already knows and will expand her vocabulary 50%.

II. BASELINE DATA : Sammie's vocabulary consists of 5 words: want, more, play. Bye and banana.

III. TECHNIQUES USED TO PROMOTE DESIRED GROWTH: Prompted with verbal cues and sign language; consistently requested Sammie to use verbal communication; reward (praise and food).

IV. END OF QUARTER DATA: Sammie has expanded her vocabulary by 100%. She has 10 words: want, more, play, banana, drink, apple, walk, open, car. Some of these words are sounds rather than the word itself. Sammie's goal was met.

PROPOSED SPECIFIC OBJECTIVE FOR NEXT QUARTER: Sammie will be more articulate in the words that she already knows and will expand her vocabulary by 50%

It has been a very successful few months. Sammie has really been changing not only with our goals, but also in other areas. She has been very aware of where she is, waiting, or coming back to me when she felt she got too far away from me. Another big change has been that since she started school her self stimulation and hyperactivity has gone way down.

My concern for Sammie is that she will be able to get the opportunity for peer group interaction as she did during the summer with the recreation department as this has been an important experience for her and all that we accomplished will be lost without it.

End of Report

<u>October 4, 1982</u>
Samantha and I will be spending a week at the Diagnostic School at Cal-State University from October 10th through October 15th. Listed below are their rules and regulations for that week.

PARENTS OF OUTSTUDENTS:

The following information is offered to assist you while living at the Diagnostic School for the week:

1. Your child will be tested and evaluated by a Pediatrician, School Psychiatrist, Diagnostic Clinic Teacher, and a Speech Hearing and Language Specialist.
2. You will be able to see and hear all of the testing sessions with your child through a one-way mirror as he/she is with the individual staff member.
3. You will not have to take your child to each scheduled appointment. Each staff member scheduled to see your child will expect to find you and child in or near the waiting area downstairs. The waiting area is in the hallway to the left as you leave the elevator downstairs. Couches and chairs are provided for your comfort should you have to wait before your child's appointment.
4. At 3 o'clock each day, the children in residence at the Diagnostic School return from their classrooms to the dormitories. At this time organized recreation begins under the direction of a professional Recreation Therapist. Your child is welcome and invited to participate in this part of the residential program should he/she so desire. It is expected that you remain with or near our child in these activities.
5. You are welcome to check out the toys, games, etc., for your child and for the week, through the Supply Room directly opposite the elevator downstairs.
6. At all times during your stay at the Diagnostic School, you are fully responsible for your child. No provision is made to "baby sit" the children. We ask you not make arrangements with other parents for the care of your child. There are three times when your child will be kept by an adult at the Diagnostic School. They are: 1) on Monday morning for the orientation meeting at 8:30;

2) while the parents are interviewed by the Psychologist; and 3) during the interview of parent(s) by the School Pediatrician.

7. All of your meals have been reserved for the number of parents (1 or 2) plus your child for the week. Should you have to change any of the reserved meals (any one of the 3 meals per day, that is, add or cancel any) the kitchen staff must be so informed the day before or earlier. Also, while in the dining room, after picking up their trays, it would be greatly appreciated if the child remains in their chairs at the table during the meal.

8. Bedroom area upstairs: at no time is there allowed any cooking of food or use of alcoholic beverages in the living quarters, bedrooms or lounge upstairs. Your bedrooms are located in the same wing with some staff offices. Please do not allow the children to play in or go unattended by a parent to the front part of the upstairs entry area, up and down the stairs, or run the elevator alone. This area is where the Business Staff, Clerical Pool. etc. are located and children will be children, noisy and distracting.

9. During the week you and your child are scheduled to be examined, tested or interviewed by the Evaluation Team between 9 am and 3 pm. There will be some time between these hours when you and your child are not scheduled. There are specified areas of the grounds and building where this time may be spent. These are: the small playground with slides, jungle gym, etc., the pool room with pool table, the Parent's Lounge upstairs with TV, and your own assigned bedroom. Please do not use the playground outside each classroom as it is distracting to the children in school. After 3 pm each day, you are welcome to leave the premises to go other places if you so desire. If you leave the premises, notify the Nurse on duty that you are leaving and approximately when you expect to return.

10. Your bedrooms are located on the second floor, main entrance to the building. At 4:30 pm each day, the two one-way glass entrance doors are locked for the night. You can only leave and enter the building on the lower floor. There is a bell to ring to re-enter on the lower floor after 5 pm.

11. It is hoped that your stay at the Diagnostic School will be a profitable one to you and your child. It may not always be a

pleasant and easy experience, but you will discover soon that the staff at the school are sincerely interested in helping you and your child to the best of their ability.

Approved: Superintendent

At the end of the first day I started what I called the Prisoner's Log:

5:30 pm Sunday, 10-10-82: Our assigned room is 6 feet wide and 8 feet long. No TV. Bathroom is adjacent – between our room (#2) and the next (#4). Sam is tearing her bed apart and checking everything out. We are due downstairs at 6:30 pm for another briefing.

11 pm to 1 am, 10-10-82: We can't sleep. The beds are as hard as the iron they are built on and they creak when we move. I can feel my joints gluing to each other and my eyes burn from crying. I wonder how Sam feels. Poor Sam!

Monday am, 10-11-82: Breakfast: watery-looking cream of wheat, scrambled eggs (?), toast. Sam refused (almost totally) to cooperate with First Tester: Karen (Communication). I ran her around school yard a half dozen laps before the second session. She cooperated beautifully with Tom (Psychologist).

Lunch: pea soup, grilled cheese sandwich, grapes. A kid vomited all over dining room!

12:30: We have no more appointments today. I haven't decided how to pass the time, but have told them we won't be here for dinner!!!

4:00 pm: We drove down Valley Boulevard to Alhambra. We will eat there at Sambo's tonight. Tried resident Phys. Ed class, but Sam "copped out" with an urgent potty call.

6:30 pm: We've made it through day #1, only 3-1/2 to go! Sambo's was the best meal we've had since we've been here!

7:00 pm: Sammie has Frog (her stuffed Froggy that is her current favorite toy) lying across her neck and ear and she is saying "night-night-night" to him. Glad he came along!

Tuesday, 10-12-82: Sam has been awake (moaning and barking, alternately) since 4 am. She didn't want juice. I curled her hair.

3:00 pm: We are done for the day. Sam never stopped moaning. She refused to cooperate with <u>anyone</u>! It was a zero day! She even "failed" Adaptive PE. Poor little kid couldn't jump on a trampoline, couldn't walk on the balance beam, etc., etc.

6:00 pm: We ate all three meals here today, although the food is so awful I couldn't eat much. I just washed and curled Sam's hair and she and frog are jumping around the room, happier than at any other time today.

Wednesday, 10-13-82: Looks like a better day. Sam is more cheerful. We are starting with Tom, Psychologist, this morning. Hopefully today she will give him a <u>cup</u> when he asks for it, not a <u>bed</u> ! Yesterday was really, really awful.

12:30: Sam is somewhat more cooperative today, but her behavior is still awful. Karen and Nancy upset me terribly by asking me "what do you want us to help you with at home" "what do you see 3 years, 10 years from now for Samantha". Tears rolled down my face all through lunch because I knew Samantha was blowing this diagnostic program with her non-compliance and would end up with a completely false diagnosis.

Physical exam next.

4:30 pm: Doctor's report and Communication "Expert" report both same as before. Irreversible brain damage and she should only be taught "functional, daily living skills". I am unrealistic and stubborn. I told them I (we) will handle the functional living skills, but as long as there is Special Education available to her, I want the school to concentrate on academic skills!

Thursday, 8:00 am 10-14-82: Sam and I sneaked out for Egg McMuffins at 7:00 am. We are feeling pretty good, but we are "hiding out" in our room to avoid questions. We are scheduled to be chauffeured to a Beverly Hills clinic at about 9:30 this morning and when we finish, we may be allowed to go home!!

<u>10-13-82</u>: INITIAL MEDICAL EVALUATION (conducted by a consulting pediatrician)

<u>CHIEF CONCERN</u>: Samantha was seen for initial medical evaluation as part of the intake process at the Diagnostic School. Background information was obtained from her mother, who was a reliable historian. In addition, medical records available in the chart were reviewed for further information.

<u>HISTORY OF PRESENT PROBLEM</u>: Mother reports that Samantha was a 9 pound 8 ounce product of a full term, uncomplicated pregnancy, with induced labor and vaginal delivery at Grand Rapids Hospital to a 37 year old gravida IV, para III, caucasion women. There were no neonatal problems and Samantha went home with her mother after two days. She seemed like a normal social and cuddly infant who fed and slept well during the first three weeks of life. However, by age three weeks, Samantha experienced low grade fever with apparent seizures and was again hospitalized at the hospital in Grand Rapids. Lumbar puncture revealed pleocytosis with elevated protein and a diagnosis of encephalitis was made. Subsequently, the mother reported that she had a different child. Motor developmental milestones remained normal, with independent sitting at five months, crawling at eight months, and walking by one year. However, behavioral and language skills were severely delayed. The mother observed none of the normal babbling, as well as a lack of interpersonal interacting. Samantha still has no purposeful speech.

Samantha was initially enrolled in a preschool program for physically handicapped at age 18 months and then began an autism program in Michigan by age three years. The family moved to California when Samantha was five years old and the parents subsequently separated and divorced. Samantha has remained in special education programs since that time, which have included programs for Trainable Mental Retardation children as well as autism. Samantha has also been in speech and language programs.

Samantha was evaluated at the Tri-Counties Regional Center by

Dr. C. in February 1982. Diagnostic studies were obtained including an EEG and CT scan. The EEG was interpreted as normal, while the CT scan showed diffused plaque-like calcifications with dilatations of the ventricle and atrophy of the temporal horn. Neurologic consultation was performed by Dr. Graham in February 1982 with diagnosis of autistic behavior syndrome and the remote history of encephalitis with mild cerebral atrophy, cerebral calcifications and ventricular dilatation as residual. There were concerns about two episodes occurring in February of this year with involuntary intermittent jerking of the left upper extremity with abnormal facial expression on the left side, possibly representing seizure activity. As noted, the EEG was normal and it was decided that he use anticonvulsant medication. The mother has observed no subsequent seizures.

PAST MEDICAL HISTORY: There have been no surgical procedures. There have been no other serious medical problems other than the possible seizures earlier this year. She is on no medication at the present time. She is allergic to bee stings.

FAMILY HISTORY: The mother is 49 years old and is healthy. The biologic father is 41 years old and reportedly has had problems with alcoholism subsequent to the parents' divorce. There are four siblings ranging in age from ten years to twenty-nine years. The mother remarried approximately 5 years ago and the stepfather has an excellent relationship with Samantha. The household constellation includes the mother, stepfather, Samantha, and her ten year old sister. Samantha has her own room. She has continued to demonstrate good motor development and she is able to roller skate and can ride on a horse.

PHYSICAL EXAMINATION: Samantha, at chronological age 11 presents as a thin Caucasian female with marked stimulatory behavior who was quite anxious about the examination procedure. Her weight is 67 pounds which is below the 10th percentile. The height is 56-1/2 inches which is at the 25th percentile. Visual acuity cannot be reliably assessed, although clinically it appears to be normal. Muscle strength is normal. Samantha was willing to balance on either foot momentarily, although I am sure she could do so for a more extended period of time. She imitated jumping up and down but never actually cleared the floor. However, she was able to do so. She would not cooperate in attempting other gross motor tasks such as hopping or skipping. There was no expressive oral language. There was much self-stimulatory behavior, intermittent hyperventilation and lack of meaningful interaction with the examiner or other people in the room.

End of report

Samantha and I were chauffeured back to the Diagnostic School and dismissed that afternoon. We high-tailed it back to Goleta as fast as we could; anxious to get back home.

October 29, 1982: The Diagnostic School was ready to report their assessment results. We asked Samantha's new teacher, Flora; a Goleta School District representative; and Kathy Hunter, Sam's case-manager from Tri-Counties Regional Center to accompany us to Los Angeles. We all got into Alan's Leisure Van and made a comfortable 100 mile journey to the Diagnostic School.

PARENT/STAFF CONFERENCE SUMMARY SHEET

Child's Name: Samantha Brown. Birth date: 4-21-71.
School District: Santa Barbara County, Hollister School

The purpose of today's conference between the Diagnostic School's staff and the above named child's parents and school district representatives was to:
1. Present the diagnostic results of the five day assessment program;
2. Discuss the primary educational needs of the child based upon the assessment findings;
3. Describe the classroom environment which can best meet the child's educational needs;
4. Discuss appropriate educational goals;
5. Discuss educational recommendations.

Recommended Educational Environment
Samantha presents with severe/profound retardation, accompanied by

many autistic behaviors and an overall atypical developmental profile. Consequently she will require a highly structured special day class with a systematic, positive, and consistent behavior management system. Program emphasis should be on the acquisition of essential skills necessary for maximum independent functioning in current and future environments. Targeted areas should include communication, social, work and life skills. Once local options are exhausted, placement in the extended diagnostic program in residence at the Diagnostic School for Neurologically Handicapped Children, Southern California, is offered to implement the program.

Recommended Related Services
Tri-Counties Regional Center
Parent Counseling
Speech and Language specialist on a consultant basis
Specially Designed P.E.

Summary of Assessment Findings
Psychological: Samantha presents with cognitive development reduced to the 2 year level. She demonstrated atypical social-affective development reduced to the 8-12 month level. During the evaluation, Samantha exhibited numerous behaviors associated with autism.
Language, Speech and Hearing: Atypical language developmental profile. Receptive language: 12 months, benefiting from a routine environment with gestural and situational cues. She has a beginning understanding of some words.
Expressional language: 12 months, using gestural cues and bodily movements to communicate wants and needs.
Educational: Fine Motor Skills: 2 year level with skill scatter; perceptual motor skills are an area of relative strength compared to dexterity and graphmotor skills.
Life Skills: Overall 2-3 year level

DISCUSSION OF FINDINGS
Throughout the week of testing, Samantha exhibited a number of behaviors which actively interfered with the evaluation. While she would generally sit in a chair on command, she typically attended very poorly to the test items. She would frequently close her eyes, did not scan

materials effectively when her eyes were open, frequently did not respond appropriately to verbal directions or commands, and exhibited a high degree of self-stimulatory behavior, during which time she was not available for learning or assessment. Samantha exhibited a wide variety of self-stimulatory behaviors. She exhibited tactile self-stimulation in which she would touch her hand to her face (usually ear or cheek) and/or at times bite her hand. She exhibited motoric self-stimulation, in which she would rock and grind her teeth. She exhibited verbal self-stimulation, in which she would make repetitious screeching vocalizations. She also exhibited visual self-stimulation, in which she would frequently stare at lights. Many of her self-stimulatory behaviors appeared to be ritualistic in nature, especially rocking. She also often repeatedly turned things over or turned them around 360 degrees in a ritualistic manner. Other behaviors she exhibited which are typically associated with autism included a general avoidance of interactions with others, avoidance of being held closely and some self-abusive behaviors (biting her hand). However, she did exhibit some behaviors which were not autistic in nature, specifically making eye contact and at times apparently enjoying having her arm or shoulder rubbed as a reinforcement. Throughout the evaluation, Samantha was very active and was very resistant to structure and direction. She did respond appropriately to a number of commands, and this appeared to be a response to the entire phrase and to other situational cues as opposed to comprehending individual words.

Various infant level tasks were structured within various environments (in the testing room, in the hallway, in the parent suite, in the classroom) to elicit both receptive and expressive language capabilities. Resistance to these activities was noted in all environments. Samantha's attention to any one task was also very fleeting. She would remain seated in a chair at a table for a prolonged period of time. Tasks were presented in a rapid and varied fashion; however, Samantha would often refuse to cooperate and would push objects onto the floor or away from her. She would also push herself away from the table or away from the examiner and rock back and forth in her chair while closing her eyes tightly with one hand on one ear and sometimes vocalize with a repetitive hum or squawk. She was easily controlled with constant attention and verbal commands such as "Sit down". At times, given a very unstructured situation in which she was to "play" Samantha would move rapidly about the room pushing things onto the floor and making a considerable amount of noise. Samantha's mother reported that Samantha's behavior at the Diagnostic School was not typical. At home, given the routine and situational cues of her environment she is able to follow directions and perform semi-independent and routine tasks. For example, the eating routine is followed on a daily basis at home. Mrs. Brown asks Samantha to get the various utensils to set the table. When she is finished eating, she is directed to take her plate outside to the trash where she scrapes off excess food and then takes her dish to the sink. Mrs. Brown also reports that Samantha will help in dressing by getting those articles of clothing as named. She also reports that Samantha can point to her facial parts upon request which was not observed during the testing situation.

End of Report

I had expected them to come up with a poor assessment due to Sam's complete lack of cooperation, but this was still shocking, devastating, and unbelievable. Fortunately, we had brought a support team of people who knew Samantha and they were as shocked as I was. This profile was NOT the Samantha that we all knew and loved!

CHAPTER TWENTY ONE;

My reaction to the diagnostic report

January 16, 1983: I wrote the following letter to my sister who lives in Michigan

"Dear Nina: When you told me that Mother doesn't always share all of my letters, I began thinking about a letter I needed to send to you to bring you up to date on Sammie's condition.

This has been my year for a reality-check (1982); the year when God (I guess) decided I was ready to face the facts. I consented to have Samantha put through the full battery of neurological testing (after 2 night-time episodes when she could not control a shaking left-hand). The results of those tests have been nicely summarized by Dr. G, who is a Consulting Pediatrician hired by the diagnostic school.

When I first became aware of Sammie's lack of proper development, I thought I could "love" the problem away. If I cuddle her enough, make hr realize how much I love her, she'll be OK. Later on I thought, it's like she's locked on the other side of a door. If I can find a way to pry open the door, she'll be OK. Then, for years, I dreamed (planned) (hoped) she would be like Anne in the book

I shared with you who steadily progressed and finally "outgrew" her illness.

Well, any or all of those are still possible, but not very probable. This does not mean that I am giving up on Sam – not in any way! But it does mean I am being more realistic about her grown up years.

When you have time, please read the entire summary of our week at the diagnostic school. Then please file it away somewhere with this letter. I am not going to ask you to be her "guardian", but I am asking you to be her "spokesperson" in case anything should happen to me.

I made a vow when she was 3 weeks old that I would always love her and care for her no matter what and I always will as long as I am able. But if anything should happen to me, the family should know what my wishes are concerning Sam.

First of all, I don't expect or want any of my children, or other relatives, to try to take on the responsibility of caring for her. I would want Sammie, with the help of an agency like Tri-Counties Regional Center, to be placed in a group home. A small one. One that would provide whatever independent living she may be capable of. "Least restrictive environment" is the phrase used. There are some of these available now and more in the planning stages as they become "tried and true".

Samantha is a dear, lovable child and she has many staunch friends in this area outside of the family circle. We have a network of people dedicated to teaching her, helping her develop to her fullest capability. It has taken time and a great deal of concern on Alan's and my part, but she is, at the moment, in an ideal circumstance, getting the best, the most informed, loving care that could possibly be provided. Getting her into the university's research program was a stroke of fortune for her. Now that Dr. K has written his book on "how to teach autistic children", her school is being used as their model. Her teacher, Flora, is working on her doctorate in special education. Her aide, Janet, who coordinates her after school programs, is her very special friend. Her speech therapist, Mary, a grad student at UCSB, spends a tremendous amount of energy on Sam 2 hours per week, trying to help her learn to speak.

Alan is a kind and loving father and he and Sam have a very special relationship. She is a fortunate little girl.

I will write a "chattier" letter soon. In the meantime, take care!
Love, Sue

P.S. After Alan read this, he criticized me for saying "if anything happened to me" – rather than "to us". His comment was that you'd "play hell" being Sam's spokesperson if he was alive and able! And he is right. By some miracle, she is his child as much as she is mine. SCB"

CHAPTER TWENTY TWO;

Meanwhile Samantha continues to make new strides forward

<u>March 15, 1983</u>

<u>Sue</u>: Flora, I thought you would like to know that your sandwich-making routine is "generalizing". Lately when Sammie is hungry, she gets out a loaf of bread and a jar of jam and brings them to us. This morning at 5 am she opened our bedroom door and said, "UP". I said, "No, Sam, it's not time to get up. Go back to your room." Ten minutes later she came back to our bedroom with a plastic bag in her hand. I got up to see what she was up to. In the kitchen, she had opened a loaf of home-made bread and stacked it neatly on a plate on the table! The jam was not available to her because we lock the refrigerator at night. Although it is 5:30 am and I am up for the day, I am very pleased with my daughter's steps toward independence and I thank you for helping her!

<u>Flora</u>: Thank you so much for your great note! I've shared it with everyone around here. It's the "little" gains that mean so much to all of us around here. And your note is very much appreciated. We teachers can always use a little positive reinforcement, too.

<u>April 21, 1983:</u> Samantha is 12 years old today

<u>Flora</u>: Happy Birthday, Sammie! Sue, thanks for the cupcakes. The class enjoyed them.

<u>June 10, 1983</u>
<u>Sue</u>: Janet, can you take care of Sammie from June 13 to 27 on a full time basis? If not, I will arrange vacation time for myself, but we are hoping to save vacation for a trip to Michigan the last two weeks in August and the first week of September.

<u>Janet</u>: Yes, I can take Sammie full time. What a coincidence in timing for August! I am getting married August 21st and will be taking a vacation the same time. If you are still in town the 21st of August, I hope you will join our family and friends for the celebration! I will send you an invitation.

<u>August, 1983</u>: Our trip to Michigan. We have taken numerous vacation trips in the Leisure Van and Samantha has learned to enjoy traveling.

Arriving at Yellowstone National Park, Wyoming

Yellowstone National Park, Wyoming

Mid Southern Nebraska

Northern Michigan

September 8, 1983: First day back to school.

Flora: Janet is officially an aide in our classroom – hooray!!

Sue: I am happy to hear that Janet is now working with you! Sammie is working harder on speech. She is putting first syllables of two words together (da – wa for drink – water); she can say ba-na-na and clearly says most of the syllables we were working on last year.

Flora sent out a little publication called "Hollister Happenings"

Wallets and ID cards :We have made a laminated ID card for each of your children. We will be teaching them to show their card when they are asked who they are. We would like to have each child keep their card in their own wallet. Therefore, (if you have not already done so) it would be really helpful if you could get your child a wallet. We also work on money and using their wallets to buy lunch, make purchases in the store, etc., so a wallet would be very helpful.

<u>Disneyland Trip</u> : We are planning a Disneyland trip on March 29th. These trips are always a lot of fun and we hope your child will be able to go.

<u>Valentine's Day</u>: We are planning a Valentine's Party on February 14th and will be exchanging Valentine cards. Below is a list of your child's classmates in case you would like to send cards. We are also including the names of your child's peer tutors (children from the Hollister regular classroom who volunteer to interact with the handicapped students).

Classmates: Sammie, John, Joey, Scott, Cherise, Kirstie, Caleb, Christina, Tanya and Erik

Peer Tutors: Cindy, Brian, Armando, Disa, Ann, Stacy, Chris, Jessica, Rayleen, Michael, Lisa, Hang, Sean, Alma, Kara, Jonna, Sara, Susan, Connie, Christine

FLORA'S CORNER
"Give Your Child A Pat on the Back"

In a recent conversation with a parent, she mentioned to me (and rightfully so) that we often overemphasize the negative and forget about the positive. For example, she already knows that her child has had a bad day in the bathroom when he comes home with a bag full of laundry. I do not need to tell her so. It really is much nicer for parents to hear some nice things that their children are doing. We all try to let you know about these, but often we take them for granted and they go unmentioned. I would like to take some time to let all of you know that your children are doing a super job! They are all really growing, taking more responsibility, communicating more, socially interacting more, and becoming independent individuals. I'd like to share just a few examples with you.

As you all know, we work on domestic jobs. Christina now takes our lunch count to the office independently every day. Erik serves our snack. Scott, Caleb, Erik and Christina are doing a great job of washing dishes. Joey and Kirstie are putting away dishes and setting the table with more and more independence. Cherise and Joey water our plants and collect trash in the yard with only a little assistance. Scott, John, and Tanya are becoming great with a broom. Sammie is really becoming independent with cooking projects. And you should see Sammie, Erik, and Christina make a bed. We also take care of our guinea pig. John, Scott, Erik and Christina have learned to feed her and clean out her cage. In all of these activities, the kids are doing a super job.

The kids are also showing a lot more communication and social interaction. In the park on our field trip Caleb and Christina were playing a chase game. Sammie plays tag with many of our peer tutors. In the morning group Scott knows the whole routine and sings all of the songs. Caleb is our little social butterfly. He knows all of the children's names and says "Hi" to everyone! Cherise is telling us many of her needs with signs and gestures. And Joey is using the "help" sign in many different situations. John is using much more speech and he can follow any direction. Tanya sings during free music time and her smile puts a spark in everyone's life. Kirstie has learned many new signs and she is using them out in the community during Social Facilitation.

We are seeing so much more independence. Cherise and Joey are walking all over by themselves. All of the children are getting off the bus by themselves and walking into class on their own. They are also eating on their own in the cafeteria. Mixed in with all the nonhandicapped children at Hollister School. Sometimes we forget and do too much for them, but when we step back and wait, it is amazing how independent they have become!

As you can see, all of your children have grown in taking responsibility, communicating, interacting socially, and being independent. We are all really proud of them and you should certainly "give your child a pat on the back!"

JANET'S CORNER

I am delighted to say I will be working another year as one of the assistants in Flora's class. Flora and I have spent many hours at Hollister already to get prepared for the new school year. We have many ideas that we have put together to fit into our new schedule for our new class. The class has grown to eight students and I think the new combination of personalities will give the class a new delightful personality. It will be a wonderful year and I can't wait to begin.

I have worked in many of the special education programs in the area and have thoroughly enjoyed every minute. Among these programs, I became very involved with one child in particular who I have worked one-on-one with for the last five years. (Sammie). It has been a great joy to see her grow and change throughout these years; to share the moments when we both gave our all to accomplish one goal; those great smiles of success will last in my heart forever. I am a true believer in "anything is possible" and if all I am is a friend to give the confidence that the children need to have confidence in themselves, then I feel very happy in giving it. I give my all and feel content that I am doing my best and that is my reward.

September 19, 1983
Sue: Our budding teenager is now using Stridex pads for her face (with Andrea's help) and Soft-n-dry deodorant.

Flora: Sammie rode her bike all alone for about 50 yards today.

Janet: Sammie and I have begun her speech therapy at Hollister School from 2:00 to 3:00. It went very well and Sammie was great. I managed to get many sounds from her with a lot of interest and excitement. We will be doing at least an hour of tactile and sensory motor activities, too.

October 4, 1983:
Sue: Sammie dressed herself totally today. I selected her clothing, but she did all the rest!

CHAPTER TWENTY THREE;

Sammie's one-to-one aide, Janet

<u>January 3, 1984</u>
<u>Sue to Flora and her aides</u>: Happy New Year and thank you for all you have done for Sammie in the old year! We (our family) thank all of you for the placemats. What a nice bit of artwork! And it is fun watching Sammie "match" the pictures. Sammie's very favorite Christmas gift is her radio headset. She has worn out 3 batteries and wears it almost continuously.

<u>January 5, 1984</u>
<u>Sue</u>: Flora, I am getting reports that Samantha is behaving very badly since school re-started. Since there is a definite, direct relationship between Sam's blood sugar level and her behavior, it might be necessary to feed her more often – especially right after vacation when she has been allowed to eat more frequently than usual.

<u>Janet</u>: We started our new goals today. I have put Sammie's wallet in her bag. Sammie goes into the grocery store with wallet in hand, picks up a banana, walks to the cashier, puts the banana on the counter, waits in line, takes money out of her wallet and gives it to cashier, then receives change, puts it in wallet, picks up bag, then outside the store she eats the banana. It worked great! Sammie had trouble keeping calm, but she will be good at this. Also, I am adding that Sammie has to unlock the door when she gets home to add more independence. We will keep the key tied to the zipper in her bag and in an inside pocket. Lastly, Samantha

is doing better at school. It just took a little while to get back into the schedule.

February 23, 1984

We had an unusual and interesting family evening between 5 and 6 pm last night. Andrea was getting help from Daddy with her math homework. Sammie joined them at the kitchen table and indicated interest. Alan provided her with paper and pencil and she sat there practicing her squiggles and circles. Two little girls vying for Daddy's attention with their homework!

January 1 through March 31, 1984

SOCIAL FACILITATION QUARTERLY REPORT
Name of Client: Samantha Brown
Name of Facilitator: Janet L

The last few months have been very difficult experiences full of growth. Sammie has done a lot of learning from her mistakes and changing herself. Sammie has been through a period of holding onto me. I have tried to pull away slowly to get her used to doing more on her own and less dependent on me; helping herself instead of asking me, and gaining the confidence that she can do things without holding onto me. It has been very difficult the last few months, but big lessons were learned.

One very big lesson Sammie learned was not to take advantage of the trust I have given her. I have given her trust and independence when she rides in my car. In the past she has done minor pranks such as turning on the windshield wipers. This quarter Sammie created a learning experience that neither of us will forget. She broke my rear view mirror not once, but three times. The first time, I talked to Sammie in a very disappointed manner, making her feel guilty but only for the moment. The second time I was very angry and let her know with loud conversation and also going home early from our beach planned day. She felt badly and cried on the way home. She was also confronted by her parents which gave the consistency that we needed, but she still needed to learn more. The third and final time, I did not say a word but remained silent all the way home and again returned home early. I could see the guilt on her face and knew the effect had been deep as she did not move an inch or make a sound.

A week later Sammie held the mirror in her hand and looked at me with look of remembrance of the weeks past, then put her hand down. I have only seen her touch the mirror one more time, but, like before, she stopped to think and returned her hand to her lap. She is delightful and I appreciate the growth and struggle she has been through.

I look back to the first day I met Sammie five years ago and see a totally different child. I remember all the experiences since that day that I have been through with her and will never forget the friendship that we have built. I am happy to be part of her life and contribute all that I can. I feel that we have crossed many bridges with much success and growth. I expect the days to come will be full of challenges and great learning experiences.

End of Report

On February 17th, 1984, we agreed to let Sammie enter the County's Special Olympics meet which will be held the first week in May. Flora and Janet have decided to enter her in the Frisbee Throw, the "long run" race event, and swimming. The volunteer coaches (students from local schools) are already working on training schedules and encouraging all the children to join the fun. The day before the big competition, we received this announcement from Flora:

THE TORCH BEARER REPRESENTING COUNTY SCHOOLS AT THE SPECIAL OLYMPICS WILL BE:

SAMANTHA BROWN

(Have her there bright and early)

That meant she would be marching in the parade in front of the County Schools banner, carrying a replica of the Olympic Games torch. Now I am nervous about Saturday!

Everything went very well. With a little coaching from Janet from the sideline, Samantha marched along with the torch held high. Well, actually, she added a few twirls which caused the television announcer to say, "Sammie appears to be a bit of a ham." Then she went on to win a blue ribbon in the race and a red (second place) in the swim-meet. We were so proud of her! Alan videotaped her from start to finish and the local cable television also taped the entire meet. The television station showed their tape a couple of weeks later and Alan was able to tape that, too.

On the 21st of May we invited Flora, Janet, and two other aides for a special showing of the Special Olympics at our house. We served Poor Boy sandwiches, wine, and soft drinks and we did a lot of laughing and cheering throughout the evening.

Samantha had her 13th birthday on April 21st, 1984, and she is progressing so well that I didn't have anything to feel sad about! Andrea is now 12 years old and is trustworthy and responsible enough to be my "back-up" babysitter. Samantha runs out of programs at about 3:30 pm and Andrea gets home from school at about 3:30, too, so the various aides and facilitators are now bringing Samantha home and Andrea watches out for her until Alan and I get home at 5:00 pm. She has become a very valuable member of Samantha's team!

April 1-June 30, 1984

SOCIAL FACILITATION QUARTERLY REPORT
NAME OF CLIENT : Samantha Brown
NAME OF FACILITATOR: Janis (Not to be confused with Janet, Samantha's best friend)

My visits with Sammie have come to be most enjoyable this first quarter together. She has a beautiful personality and disposition. We have done many activities together and because of our previous acquaintance through her school, she immediately felt at ease with me.

We started with a laundry objective and she enjoys this environment. The goals were (1) take laundry basket out of car; (2) walk into Laundromat ; (3) put dirty clothes in washer; (4) put detergent in washer; (5) deposit money in machine and start; (6) when washer stops, take out clothes and put in dryer; (7) deposit money and start machine; (8) take clothes out of dryer; (9) fold clothes. (10) Put clothes basket in car.

There is enough stimulus provided for her that she attends to the task at hand.

We have done speech work at my house and she has taken a liking to my cats. When she first met them, she began to make sounds and, with help, she formed the word "cat", followed by a giggle. She now picks them up and carries them around the house upon arrival.

We did some practicing for her special moment at the Special Olympics. As torch bearer, she was proud and excited.

We have also gone bowling and played hiball. Both of these activities held her interest and she became quite pleased with her ability to play the games. These will be definitely continued activities in the future.

Tactile sessions have also been included in our outings. Sammie is much better behaved with these sessions. Her senses seem alleviated temporarily with this stimulation. The sessions include piling sand on her body when we are at the beach and rubbing her back and arms with a brush. Sometimes she gets to put her feet in a foot massager which is also relaxing for her.

As Sammie and I get to know each other outside of the school setting, our friendship seems to be headed to the trustworthy stage. I am becoming familiar with her likes and dislikes as well as what motivates her the most.

End of Report

Janet and Janis are also working on another objective that isn't going as well. They take turns taking her into a grocery store to buy a banana for snack time. Samantha has needed many prompts through each of the steps. Sammie had a very hard time controlling herself and needed a lot of discipline. Some of the bad days included things like knocking over a display of bottles and one time, when waiting in line, she knocked a lady's groceries out of her hand. Both Janis and Janet were very consistent with discipline and Samantha did eventually meet their objectives.

Flora held an Open House for parents and students on the 3rd of May, 1984. On the 7th of May, I wrote the following letter to her with a copy to the President of the Goleta School Board:

"Dear Flora: I want to thank you again for the marvelous slide show presentation you and your staff put together for Open House last Friday evening. It was not only fun for all the parents to see the children, but also very informative.

For the first time since we have been in California, I am relaxed and confident about Samantha's education. It has felt like a long, hard struggle but finally in your classroom she is getting exactly the program she needs. Your teaching method is exemplary, innovative, tailored to each child's need – it was very impressive! I sincerely hope you are receiving the recognition you deserve for the program you have built and for the progress the children are making under your tutelage.

"Thank you" does not begin to express the gratitude we feel!

Sincerely, Sue and Alan"

September 19, 1984: Hooray! Samantha is starting a speech class at UCSB again! It will begin this Saturday with Kathy D. Both Janet and Janis volunteered to give Kathy any input they could and/or sit in on the first session. Flora said to be sure to have Kathy call her to let her know what she was doing in order to be consistent. With everybody on "the same page", I am really looking forward to more improvement in Sammie's speech.

September 22, 1984 Kathy D's first report: "Sammie did really well in speech. We played with a lot of toys and I would have her verbalize for the toys which she did consistently. The session was mostly to see what kinds of activities she liked to do and what her verbal repertoire was. She is quite communicative, lots of eye contact and turn-taking abilities. Janis and Janet can come any Saturday they would like to and if they would like to call me we could discuss some things about Sam, such as what to do about hitting. Today I would briefly restrain her by holding her wrist for a few seconds and say "no hitting". She also was trying to communicate with me with sign language, but I didn't understand it. I would like to know what her signs are so that I could respond to her attempts to communicate."

<u>October 5, 1984</u>: Janis wrote the following note in Samantha's journal: "Kathy, Sammie did some good speech work with me at the beach today. I would like to observe your next session. Here is a list of items Sammie prefers (1) Any tactile things – sand, beans, rice, shaving cream, and clay; (2) Musical toys or instruments; (3) Bubbles; (4) Balls; (5) Squeaky toys; (6) Music – radio and tapes.

<u>October 19, 1984</u>: Flora has invited parents and kids to another Open House. Janis and Samantha are going to shop at the grocery store for ingredients to make cookies to take to the meeting. I was in for a big surprise that evening!

<u>October 22</u>: A letter from me to Flora, Janet and Janis: "Thanks for a great evening Friday. It was such an uplift for me to find Sam's eye-hand coordination has improved enough for to thread a needle! Her smile when she put that necklace on me is stored away in my memory as a <u>real treasure</u>!

CHAPTER TWENTY FOUR :

Sammie's Bus Riding Behavior

School Year 1985-1986

Samantha's bus-riding behavior has never been very good. She has always hated being strapped into her seat and always managed to annoy the driver one way or another. When she was a little girl her bad behavior was tolerated; as she got older various methods were employed to keep her under control. One method was having her wear headphones with music and that kept her relatively compliant. Now, however, she is a full-grown teenager who still hates those little yellow buses and her behavior toward the drivers is deteriorating. One substitute driver (a huge man, at least 6 feet tall and weighing about 400 pounds) declared that Sammie had hit him and he had to go on Workers Compensation! It had come to a point where she was no longer welcome to ride on the bus. Kathy H. (Sammie's caseworker from Tri-Counties Regional Center) arranged funding for a Behavior Specialist to ride with Sam for a period of 3 months (5/16/85 to 8/1/85).

Sam's behaviors on the bus included spitting, screaming, aggression toward the driver, and unfastening her seat belt. Self-injurious behavior was defined as pinching herself, banging her head against the bus seat, or biting her hand or arm. Aggression was defined as any instance of kicking, hitting, pinching, or throwing objects at another person or in the direction of another person. Disruptive behavior was defined as any emission of noise above the normal talking range (shrieks, yells, wails) and rocking in a sideways motion so far that she is at a 45 degree angle to her bus seat.

Joy, the Behavior Specialist, spent the next three months teaching the bus drivers how to deal with Samantha's behavior and it began to pay off, bringing peace to the driver and the other children.

Notes from Joy began to appear in Sam's journal: "Sammie did very well, 23 minutes with no spitting; Morning ride we used harness (I had designed a vest that fastened over the seat belt that kept Sam in her seat and covered the buckle so she could not unfasten it); afternoon was great; she didn't need the headphones today; fantastic rider with new driver, etc.,"

April 12, 1985: The Goleta School District and Kathy H. of Tri-Counties Regional Center recommended that Samantha Brown be evaluated for Occupational Therapy. I received the following information from the Saratoga Clinic for Pediatric Therapy:

"Present Level of Functioning: Samantha tends to seek out tactile exploration and has a strong drive for propioceptive (muscle/joint) input, (pinches, bites, hits self). This behavior has especially increased since Samantha reached puberty. Samantha tends to crave spinning activities, swinging high and sitting and rocking.

The above behaviors were observed during occupational therapy screening assessment. Her behavior was very repetitive with a strong need to seek out tactile and sensory stimulation. Her need to seek out movement stimulation was not as strong. She did frequently seek out repetitive rocking.

Recommendations: Occupational therapy treatment 2 times per week to determine, in depth, Samantha's treatment needs. Treatment should be directed towards helping to normalize tactile, propioceptive and vestibular sensory systems. Goals should be directed also toward helping her seek out tactile and proprioceptive input through more socially acceptable means. Classroom consultations to help teachers meet Samantha's sensory needs in the classroom.

Re-evaluate in 3 months to determine the need to continue therapy and, if so, to continue to review goals."

Samantha was not at all interested in "OT" and spent most of her time resisting instead of cooperating, but finally, about 6 months later the reports began to improve. They began working together in June and by November Samantha would initiate getting on the equipment and maintain a prone position while experiencing movement. The OT therapist reported that her need to self-stimulate had decreased and she had improved basic motor skills and improved physical fitness. She said, "A lot of work was done with mats: rolling, crawling, and jumping and Samantha seemed to enjoy all of these."

For 1985 Samantha's classroom objectives were: (1) Improve co-operation and following instructions in group activities; (2) Improve independent community skills and community awareness (a) bus riding skills; (b) aware of safety signs; (c) purchasing items in stores. (3) Improve domestic skills in the areas of washing dishes and setting the table.

Instead of using Samantha's journals, the school staff started sending "Weekly Summary Sheets" to report Samantha's activities. My last journal entry was made on September 15, 1985, "Our household now has a dog named "Flower"! She is a big, gentle Siberian Husky who snatches Sam's socks while she's trying to put them on and makes her giggle."

WEEKLY SUMMARY SHEET
COGNITIVE

Monday: Sammie worked on matching objects. She initially had problems matching, but I think she was just "goofing around". Then she matched identical objects with 100% accuracy. She also worked on imitating hand raising and nose touching also with 100% accuracy.

Tuesday: Sammie said "ma" and signed music. She listened to music for doing good work.

Wednesday: I tried working with Sammie one on one asking yes or no questions. Sam preferred to act dumb. She would not touch the right body parts – only her ears.

Thursday: Sammie worked well. She talked a lot and then when repeating the alphabet sounds, she did 50% (A-P) without any physical prompts.

Friday: Sammie has the ability to say almost all the letters in the alphabet. She did it today with beautiful sounding "la" and "ma".

PRE-VOCATIONAL

Monday: Sammie started her work very quietly, but as we got further into the task, she began playing games. She packaged 4 items, labeled and stapled. Still has difficulty putting on label, but knows what comes next. Stuffing envelopes by color. Needed verbal prompts to match envelope.

Tuesday: Pen assembly. Didn't follow assembly left to right. Stuffing envelopes by color – goofed off and didn't look at work.

Wednesday: Samantha worked on packaging nuts and bolts. She was unable to work independently, except for putting the folded paper over the plastic envelope.

Thursday: Samantha worked on packaging 2 blocks in a tube. She was very noncompliant and tantrumed throughout.

Friday: 3 pens to assemble. Waited or goofed off until pointed out which part was next, although she knows. Nut and bolt assembly – finished four after several prompts.

DOMESTIC
Monday: Sammie is taking care of "Pat", the guinea pig this week. At the beginning he would squeal when she came near because she handled him very roughly.

Tuesday: Sammie cupped her hands to pick Pat up and was much more at ease with him. She needed verbal prompts to take out dirty paper, put in clean, give him food and physical prompts to change the water.

Wednesday: Sammie and Pat had a better day. She picked him up so nice and I prompted her to pet him after she put him down. She then independently changed the paper and needed gestures for the food. She still needed physical prompts for the water. Unscrewing the top has become quite an ordeal and she gets frustrated. After she finishes she has been giving him a carrot. She loves this part – a reward for both of them!

Thursday: Samantha is still cleaning Pat's cage. She now knows the steps and picks up Pat carefully. She is even spontaneously petting her. She can do all the steps with verbal prompts only, except laying the paper flat in the cage and removing the top to the water bottle. So nice to see her show increased interest in our pet!

Friday: Sam cleaned Pat's cage again today. She was quite quick at doing it and my direct verbal prompts have faded to indirect. She again handled Pat so nicely and <u>Pat no longer screams when she sees Sam coming!</u> Good work, Sam!

<u>November 26, 1985</u> Flora wrote an Annual Review for the County Superintendent of Schools.

Student: Samantha Brown
Classroom Teacher: Flora B.

Annual Goal: Expand level of independence in domestic tasks. Samantha has made excellent progress in this area. She is able to completely wash and dry her hands at a 95% level of independence. She only requires an occasional reminder to get all the dirt off. She is able to wash her hair in the shower at the pool. She is able to follow picture recipes to prepare simple food items with a 70% level of independence. She has begun to learn to make the bed and, with some monitoring, she can complete the task at a 75% level of independence. She is able to dress independently within ten minutes. She has learned to thread a needle and stitch along the edge of a pattern to sew simple items. She has learned to clean and feed the guinea pig at an 80% level of independence. She is able to water the plants at a 95% level of independence.

At this time domestic goals should be oriented towards increasing independence and expanding her repertoire of skills.

Annual Goal: Continue to develop more independent and appropriate community skills.

Samantha has also made good progress in this area. She has learned to be quiet and behave appropriately on the bus, in stores and at other public places. She is able to use her wallet identification to identify herself with 80% consistence. She is able to use her wallet to pay for an item with 90%

independence. She is able to use a washing machine at the Laundromat with a 70% level of independence.

At this time community skills should be oriented towards increasing appropriate public behavior and increasing independence in community activities.

Annual Goal: Continue to develop social and communication skills in leisure time activities. Choose appropriate activities.

Samantha has made progress in this area. She has learned to take turns and wait while participating in group games. She has participated in board games with her classmates and peer tutors. She has learned to choose leisure activities in the yard (skating, swinging, jumping and climbing) however, she continues to have a difficult time staying away from the dirt and grass.

At this time, there should be an emphasis on choosing appropriate leisure time skills with the use of her picture wallet.

Annual Goal: Continue to develop pre-vocational and pre-cognitive skills.

This has been a more difficult area for Samantha. She seems to do better with functional activities. She has learned some packaging tasks and one-to-one correspondence. She has also learned to discriminate the difference between twist and push tops on pens and a variety of containers. She is able to cut at designated lengths. We have also exposed her to a job at Wendy's Restaurant. She is sweeping up trash in the parking lot and she is doing an excellent job. However, the area of pre-cognizant skills presents difficulty for Sammie. She has learned to trace SAM, but she has a great deal of difficulty when no model is present. It seems more appropriate that Samantha's fine motor skills be directed toward leisure skills such as art. Also, she may benefit from doing art activities on the computer. She was introduced to the computer this year by a university student and this did not go well; however, more exposure would probably be appropriate. Samantha has also had a great deal of difficulty with imitating the sounds of the letters. On certain days, she is able to get many of the sounds, but on other days she is very frustrated and the goal of 80% consistency was not achieved. She seems to do much better with picture card communication.

At this time it is recommended that vocational skills be taught in the community at actual job site. Communication should be expanded through the use of a picture wallet. The use of the computer as a leisure time activity should be explored more.

Conclusions: Samantha has had a very good year. She seems to do well with functional activities. It is recommended that she continue to work on increasing independence and expanding her repertoire of skills in the domestic, community, leisure and vocational areas. Since she is 14-1/2 years old, it is also recommended that Samantha move to our adolescent program at La Colina Junior High School effective January 1986.

August 6, 1986 : Letter from Santa Barbara Recreation Department:

> "Dear Sue: I am sorry things didn't work out for Sam this year. The group has drastically changed from the past. Most of our autistic teens have left the area. Sam's old group has been replaced by two groups of younger children.
>
> I don't want to fail Sam completely. We have two activities that Sam was very successful in: swimming and horseback riding. We have Ortega Pool to ourselves on Tuesdays and Thursdays and horseback riding Thursdays from 1:00 to 2:00 at the Olive Tree Ranch.
>
> Andrea is welcome to bring Sam to any of those activities. No further contact needs to be made, we are there and welcome Sam at any time. Andrea could bring her, stay with her, and return her home.
>
> Sincerely,
> Recreation Supervisor"

CHAPTER TWENTY FIVE;
La Colina Junior High School

<u>September 1986</u> : Samantha is being transferred to her 5th school. In addition to the setbacks she goes through in adjusting to a new school, she is losing Flora who has been the very best teacher she has ever had. She is also losing Janet and Janis.

Janet decided to attend university and get a degree in teaching handicapped children. We are sad to lose her (after 6 years of working with Samantha), but she is doing the right thing and we are very proud of her. Below is a reference letter we wrote for her:

TO WHOM IT MAY CONCERN:

Janet L. has been a large factor in our handicapped (autistic) daughter's life for the past six years. Their relationship began when Janet worked for the Santa Barbara Recreation Department and Samantha went to Develcamp. Since then Janet has worked with Sam in a variety of jobs; she was an aide with the Upjohn Home Care Service and provided after school care while I worked; she was a Social Facilitator with Tri-Counties Regional Center working on specific goals toward helping Samantha fit into the community; and for the past two years, she has worked as a teacher's aide in Samantha's classroom at Hollister Special Education Center.

Janet taught Sammie to tie her shoes, working from an

8-step hierarchy process, painstakingly teaching her one step at a time; she taught her to swim and to ride a two-wheel bicycle. She often acted as Samantha's program coordinator, being the go-between who provided transportation, supervision and monitoring programs Samantha could not have been involved in (because of a working mother) if Janet had not stepped in. One of the most significant of these was the speech therapy at the University of California at Santa Barbara. Samantha learned to approximate syllables; Janet learned to teach and promote speech in children who have not mastered normal speech.

Listing all of these activities may make them sound simple, but Samantha's neurologically symptomatic behaviors always stood between Janet and her objectives and each goal was a hard won battle. Had it not been for Janet's tenacity, patience and loving care, Sammie might not have achieved any of these goals.

I am not surprised that Janet is seeking to broaden her experience and knowledge; she is only continuing down a road she set foot on some time ago. She is that rare and special person who is innately qualified to deal with handicapped children.

There are not enough superlatives to describe our appreciation for Janet's involvement in Samantha's life. She is Samantha's best friend!

Suzanne C. Brown (Sam's mother)
Alan F. Herboldsheimer (Sam's dad)

September 15, 1986: We received the letter below from the new teachers:

"Dear Parents/Guardians:

After tossing around several ideas, we have arrived

at a new home communication format. Our goal in developing the current system is to provide you with a systematic, concrete, individualized daily progress report. The foundation depends on your student's yearly IEP (Independent Education Program) goals. We have briefly listed each goal, leaving a blank for the specific criterion level. This allows us to set short term objectives/goals for each month. If at any time during that month, the criterion is met, the level will be raised. If at the end of the month, the criterion has not been met, we will reevaluate the program and adjust accordingly. When a percentage score is available it will be recorded; when not available, a check mark will represent that training has taken place on that particular day.

Following each progress report, you will find a comment page. In the left column daily comments, regarding student appearance, attitude and/or achievement, will be recorded. The right hand column is for your comments. We find your responses valuable and encourage you to record them on a daily basis.

Sincerely yours
Beth M. and Sharen E.

SHORT TERM OBJECTIVES
Samantha will be able to:
1. Prepare a simple meal at 50% independence for 2 out of 3 consecutive sessions. i.e. grilled cheese, soup, toast
2. Operate a new kitchen appliance at 50% independence for 2 consecutive sessions. i.e. microwave
3. Perform one new domestic skill at 50% independence for 2 out of 3 sessions. i.e. vacuum
4. Select a physical education, recreation, or leisure activity, obtain materials, and use appropriately for at least 5 minutes with 70% independence
5. Will have the opportunity to engage in age-appropriate physical education or leisure activity, 30 minutes once a week

6. Select, order and purchase an item in a community environment at 25% independence for 2 out of 3 sessions

7. Will have the opportunity to engage in at least 2 local community environments

8. Participate in community environment for at least 10 minutes, behaving appropriately.

9. Expressively use and receptively understand at least one new signs. i.e. "help"

10. Appropriately request desired items through the use of signs/pointing at 50% independence for 2 out of 3 sessions

11. Work continuously for at least 3 minutes at 50% independence in vocational training

12. Perform at least 2 new vocational skills at 70% independence for 2 out of 3 sessions.

<u>September 29. 1986</u> : Samantha started behaving badly on the bus again. She threw her shoes at the driver and unbuckled her seatbelt. It was determined that she could not ride on the bus until Tri-Counties was able to provide an Intensive Behavior Intervention person again. It would be a few weeks before the service could begin, so I had to pay the consequences. I had to drive Samantha to school and she wasn't allowed to arrive before 9 am. I also had to pick her up at 3 in the afternoon and take her home. Andrea was home from school by the time Samantha and I arrived, so she took care of her until Alan got home at about 5:05 pm. My bosses at Santa Barbara Research Center were very understanding, but I still felt I had to make up the hours I was missing (a total of 3 hours per day). I worked until 7 pm for the 3 weeks that Samantha needed remedial training in bus behavior.

By the end of October the reports about her bus behavior were better: "Sam was super on the bus today", "Sam got off the bus without being prompted", etc. I just hope she keeps it up!

Her behavior at school was surprisingly "normal" for her. She had made the transition to the new school and the loss of her friends without the usual setbacks. Beth and Sharen were good teachers and appeared to know how to handle an autistic teenager.

Notes from school varied from day to day. This is the week of October 22nd to 26th:

<u>Monday</u>: Sam was able to swim today. She was good in the water and super dressing herself.

<u>Tuesday</u>: Sam had an OK morning, but was wild after lunch. She ran one mile on the track and then hit another student. She was brought back to class to do a task and then to the dressing room to change. She is doing well in the locker room. She is dressing and undressing faster and more appropriately. She dresses after other students leave for now until she gets used to the routine.

<u>Wednesday</u>: Sam had a good day, especially taking into account all the rain. She made soup for lunch – great for a dreary day.

<u>Thursday</u>: Sam went shopping today and got her money out of her wallet very well.

<u>Friday</u>: Flora was substituting for Sharen today. Sam enjoyed seeing her!

<u>October 17, 1986</u> :
ANNUAL REPORT 1985-1986
STUDENT: Samantha Brown
AGE: 15 years, 6 months
CLASSROOM INSTRUCTOR: Beth M

<u>Annual Goal</u>: To increase independence and accuracy of domestic skills

Samantha has made excellent progress in this area. She is able to obtain necessary materials, prepare two slices of toast or frozen waffles, and clean up with 80% independence for two consecutive sessions. Samantha is able to put away clean dishes in kitchen cabinets and fold clean laundry with 70% independence for 2 out of 3 sessions. She has had the opportunity to make a variety of meals using various kitchen appliances. At this time she is able to independently operate a toaster at 100% independence and a blender and microwave at 70% independence when aided in programming correct time for cooking and blending.

Recommendation: At this time domestic should be oriented towards increasing independence and expanding her repertoire of skills in preparing her own lunch.

Annual Goal: To continue to develop more independent and appropriate community skills.

Samantha has had the opportunity to engage in at least two different community environments at least two times a week. She has experienced training in shopping skills at a local 7-11 convenience store in which she is able to walk to and from to purchase needed items to prepare her lunch. She is able to use her wallet during money transactions at 50% independence. Samantha also has the opportunity to take part in a bowling program at San Marcos Lanes 1 to 2 times per week. At this time her social behavior is quite sporadic which inhibits her from intense community training.

Recommendation: At this time community skills should be oriented towards increasing appropriate public behavior and increasing independence in money transactions and shopping skills.

Annual Goal: To continue to develop independence and accuracy of physical education, recreation and leisure skills.

Using her picture communication book, Samantha is able to page through the photographs of leisure/free time activities and choose an activity of her choice, obtain materials needed, and use appropriately for at least 15 minutes with 80% independence. At this time Samantha regularly chooses a radio and headphones. Samantha has the opportunity to engage in an age-appropriate physical education class on a daily basis. She enjoys swimming, jogging, and skating. She is able to jog and skate at least five miles while still asking for "more".

Recommendation: At this time there should be emphasis on allowing Samantha to engage in a daily rec/leisure activity of her choice. Intensive studies have shown that Samantha's inappropriate behavior decreases when allowed to release excess energy through appropriate means (i.e. physical education).

Annual Goal: To develop and increase communication skills.

Samantha is able to receptively understand pictures in her communication book, but requires prompting to independently use the book to express needs and desires. Sam will spontaneously sign "work", "drink", and "bathroom". Samantha has been working on the sign "help", but confuses it with "work" due to the fact that they are quite similar in physical structure.

Recommendation: At this time Sam should increase her communication skills by continuing to use her communication picture book to spontaneously express her needs and desires. I recommend she also continue to learn "coping" signs (i.e. "help", "finished", "please", etc.) to be used during natural occurrences in both classroom and community environments.

Annual Goal: To develop and increase independence of vocational training skills

Samantha's excessive aberrant behavior during transportation and at work training site has inhibited her from receiving vocational training in the community.

Recommendation: In that Sam is only fifteen years old, she still has several years of education ahead of her. It is my recommendation that Samantha concentrates on increasing her appropriate behavior in the classroom and community prior to receiving vocational training.

CONCLUSIONS: Samantha has had a good year. She has weathered the multiple changes in staff and school environments. It is recommended that she continue to work on increasing independence and expanding her repertoire of skills in the domestic, community, rec/leisure, and communication areas. In addition, it is recommended that she increase her independence in self-help skill, specifically in dressing and undressing and using appropriate table manners when eating meals."

End of Report

October 25, 1986 :
Sue: Alan had surgery yesterday and will be in the hospital 5 days. Samantha misses him.

October 28, 1986 :
Sue: You all may not believe this, but, trust me, it's too important to exaggerate! Do you recall me telling you Sam has an "emergency language"? Well, this morning Sam was whining and I said, "What's the matter, Sam?" and she said, "Wa Da-dee"(her equivalent of "Want Daddy") in a loud, clear voice. The only other time I've heard her say Da-dee (2 syllables together) was when she had set the kitchen on fire! She really misses Alan. He will be home Sunday.

Beth: Yay! Super news both in Sam's speech and Alan coming home.

November 11, 1986 :
Sue: I'm going to Michigan for a week (12th to 19th November) so Alan and Andrea will be in charge.

November 19, 1986 :
Beth : Real rough day for Samantha! She pulled out all of her old tricks on the bus including throwing her shoes out of the window. Sorry!! She did lots of spitting and spent the entire afternoon washing tables due to excessive spitting. Nice welcome home, huh!?

November 20, 1986 :
Michigan was very cold and snowy. It's great to be home! Samantha was due for new shoes anyway. I thought she had forgotten that trick! Hope she behaves better today.

November 25, 1986:
Beth : Samantha was absolutely wonderful at shopping today at 7-11. She bought butter for grilled cheese and a coke for good work. Not a peep out of her.

December 15, 1986 : Another school location change for Samantha! This will be the 6th campus change for her.

Dear Parents and Guardians: We would like to let you know that on January 5th (after Christmas vacation) our classes will be separated. Our second instructional site will be held at Work Incorporated at 330 State Street. Beth's class will be at Dos Pueblos High School on Monday, Wednesday and Fridays, and at Work Inc. on Tuesdays and Thursdays. Sharen's classes will run on the opposite schedule; Monday, Wednesday and Friday at Work Inc and Tuesdays and Thursdays at Dos Pueblos.

We are all looking forward to our new classroom facility. It will give us the opportunity to develop more job sites in that Work Inc not only employs disabled adults, but its central location allows for a higher intensity of community integration. This move will allow for training to take place within potential and future environments in which your son or daughter may engage after graduation.

We are anxious to have you visit us at our new location and would like to take this opportunity to invite you to our Open House on January 27th at Work Inc.

We encourage you to give us a call if you have any questions. Until then we wish you and your family a Merry Christmas.

Sincerely,
Beth and Sharen

This news was followed by a letter to me from Work Training Program, Inc:

Dear Mrs. Brown:

As you know, Work Training Program, Inc. has been asked by Tri-Counties Regional Center to assume sponsorship of the Social Facilitation Program in which your child participates.

We believe that the services offered by this program are excellent and should continue without disruption to the families involved.

WTP's principle responsibilities involve administration of the program and supervision of the Facilitators who work directly with the clients.

Our intention is to insure that the assessment of your child's needs, the program plan to meet those needs, and the teachers who carry out those plans are uniformly excellent.

As a means of getting acquainted with each other, we would like to invite you to a Parent's Night Coffee here at WTP. At that time we can properly introduce ourselves, exchange ideas and generally share information with each other.

Sincerely,
Stephen M.
Resource Developer

This organization was very well known for training mental retarded people and finding employment for them. Because Samantha had never developed useable speech, I could not imagine sending her out to work in her adult years. In addition to that, she never was a calm and compliant student. Her autistic behaviors always got in the way of most of the tasks that were required of her. Below is her first week in this program:

Monday: Samantha had two pens to assemble. She threw the rings on the floor, so she lost one before beginning the task. After that she assembled them almost independently, but needed prompts to stay on task.

Tuesday: Samantha was set up with two pens to assemble and once again lost the rings. After she looked for them (and they are really gone), we gave her a new set and she settled down and put them together entirely on her own.

<u>Wednesday</u>: Sammie tried a new packaging sequence with different sized plastic bottles. She was to put an item in the bottle and then put the lid on. She figured it out quickly, but played around with the items. She completed the job with numerous verbal prompts.

<u>Thursday</u>: Samantha had a bin of mixed items to assemble. She was horrible! She knows how to construct all of the items, but whined and tantrumed and put wrong combinations together. She completed 3 out of 7 in a half hour.

<u>Friday</u>: Samantha was to sort and stuff envelopes with two colors. She did not attend to task, tried to get out of working.

As I suspected, Samantha was not a candidate for employment with Work, Inc! The good news, however, is that the move to yet another campus did not upset Samantha. She continued to respond to Beth's teaching methods and maintained her growths.

<u>PROGRESS REPORT FOR SCHOOL YEAR 1987</u>

<u>Major Objectives</u>
To increase and develop recreational and leisure skills:
1. Samantha will have the opportunity to participate in at least two weekly age-appropriate community activities. (Achieved)
2. With verbal directions, Samantha will be able to rotate among three stations and perform the appropriate exercises, using an exercise bicycle and other physical education equipment with 70% independence for 2 out of 3 sessions. (Achieved)
3. With no more than 4 verbal reminders to stay on task, Samantha will be able to run alongside a staff member or non-handicapped peer for at least 1 mile on a campus or non-campus track with 100% independence for 2 consecutive sessions.(Achieved)

To increase and develop communication skills:

1. Samantha will be able to spontaneously use the signs "help" and "finished" in appropriate situations with 50% independence for 2 out of 3 sessions. (Achieved)

Samantha had a truly fantastic session. She seemed to really be enjoying the activities she took part in and, therefore, her aberrant behavior literally disappeared. By the end of the session she was jogging and skating at least 5 miles and still begging for more. It was a real pleasure working with her.

Teacher: Beth M.

The second half of the 1987 school year was as successful as the first:

EXTENDED SCHOOL YEAR PROGRESS REPORT

Major Summer Session Objectives:

1. Samantha will have the opportunity to participate in at least two different age-appropriate recreation/leisure activities (i.e. Swimming, skating, jogging, jazzercize) on a daily basis for a 60 minute duration.

Achievement: On a daily basis Samantha participated in at least one of the following activities: jogging, skating, basketball and/or jazzercize.

2. Samantha will be able to maintain her present level of 75% independence to prepare a simple meal (toast, refrigerated muffins toaster waffles, blender fruit drink) for two consecutive sessions.

Achievement: Upon verbal request, Samantha was able to obtain the necessary materials and prepare toast and/or fruit blender drink with 82% accuracy for two consecutive sessions.

3. When asked to change or get dressed Samantha will be able to maintain her present ability of 77% independence for two consecutive sessions to occur during natural settings (i.e. PE).

Achievement: During PE Samantha was required to dress in sweats prior to work-out. With no more than two verbal prompts to stay on task, Sam was able to fully dress/undress herself for three consecutive sessions.

I was thoroughly impressed with both Samantha's attitude and behavior during the extended school year. She was extremely responsive to both her peers and staff. Sam utilized both her receptive and expressive communication skills to their fullest. She was attentive, determined and a pleasure to work with.

Teacher: Beth M.

Our personal life hit an unpleasant little bump in August of 1987. We had a back-fence neighbor who had annoyed us for years because he didn't like the noise she made. He was a cantankerous old man who was unhappy with many of his neighbors. He trapped cats and disposed of them and, if a dog left a "calling card" in his front yard, he would scoop it up and dump it close to the neighbor's front door. One time I heard our teen-age neighbor sobbing and pleading with him to give her cat back. He refused to do so because he said the cat had "peed on his lettuce"! Several times he had called Alan over to the back fence and railed at him for having brought Samantha into the neighborhood. I knew from these exchanges that he put Samantha in the same category as the cats. He often had his wife telephone us and say that he couldn't stand Sam's noise for one more minute. Every time that happened, we brought Sam into the house. One time she called and said Samantha had been making noise all weekend; however, we had been away all weekend and had just arrived home when she called.

At this particular time Samantha was at home from 3 p.m. until we got home from work at 5:15. Apparently he decided to escalate his complaints. I got a phone call at work from Andrea informing me that a representative from Children's Protective Service had come to the house and had left her card and wanted me to call her. I telephoned her immediately and made an appointment with her for the next day. Alan and I were both at home when she came to the house the next day. Her letter that summed up her investigation is quoted below:

"Our office received a complaint on July 20, 1987, stating

that Samantha Brown is autistic and that she is put outside at 8:00 am and left outside until 8:00 pm and that she screams all day long. They further stated that there is a teenage daughter in charge of Samantha and the reporting source feels that this teenager can't handle Samantha due to the fact that Samantha is getting bigger, can't talk, and screams all the time. The reporting source feels the parents are able to afford to hire someone to care for Samantha instead of the teenage daughter. The reporting source feels that the parents do not want Samantha in the house. The reporting source had contacted the Sheriff's office who forwarded the complaint to Child Protective Service.

An attempted home visit was made by me. I spoke with a teenage girl who was babysitting and then Samantha's sister who returned to the home while I was there. I left my card and Mrs. Brown called me as soon as she received it. An appointment was made for the next day.

I spoke with Suzanne Brown, Alan Herboldsheimer, their teenage daughter, the babysitter, and observed Samantha. After the history of the situation, past problems with neighbors and talking with Samantha's social worker from Tri-Counties Regional Center, it is my professional judgment that this child, Samantha, is receiving exceptional care and supervision; she is benefiting from every available service and resource in this community. Samantha is doing remarkably well in the home environment. This child is profoundly handicapped and the entire family is to be commended for the work they have done with this her to help her function as well as she does.

The case was closed. The allegations were unfounded.

Sincerely,
Carolyn K.
Children's Protective Services

Alan and I decided that enough was enough with this man and consulted an attorney to see what could be done. . The attorney suggested that a strongly worded letter would be a good place to start. Alan said, "OK and put in the word "despicable". The attorney's letter is quoted below:

"Dear Sir: The undersigned represents Alan Herboldsheimer and Suzanne Brown in connection with the below-described matter. Future correspondence or communications with respect to this matter should be addressed to the undersigned.

You have recently made complaints to government agencies concerning Samantha Brown, Ms. Suzanne Brown's daughter. You have alleged that lack of care is being provided to the minor child Samantha. Such complaints are false. Since you have involved government agencies and third persons, your conduct is defamatory and is actionable.

Further, you have engaged in a course of conduct over a period of years which has been calculated by you to invade the privacy of Mr. Herboldsheimer and Mrs. Brown and, by your conduct, we can only conclude that you have intended to cause them embarrassment and distress. My clients have begun to tire of your puerile attitude and will no longer tolerate it.

As you know, you live in an urban society in which the needs and interests of different members of the community sometimes conflict with each other. My clients are sorry if you feel inconvenienced in any way by the reasonable activities they undertake on their property. However, your vexatious response to members of your neighborhood, including my clients, is exceedingly inappropriate.

I urge you to consult with an attorney concerning the

meaning and consequences of engaging in activity constituting defamation of character and invasion of privacy as such conduct is actionable and may result in the imposition of money damages against you. I am sure some independent legal advice would be of some assistance to you in guiding your future conduct.

I expect that I will have no further complaints from my clients concerning your conduct. If I am contacted again, you may anticipate a prompt and effective response.

Kindly guide yourself accordingly as no further notice prior to the filing of an action will be provided.

Regards,
Kenneth F., Attorney at Law"

Alan and I agreed that the attorney's letter was well written and would probably take care of the matter, but I was still very angry and wanted the man to receive some immediate punishment. I wrote the following letter to our local Elks Lodge:

"Dear Exalted Ruler:

You and I have a problem: one of your brothers, a member of Elks Lodge XXX, has (for more than 5 years) been harassing a handicapped child, my daughter Samantha Brown.

Samantha had viral encephalitis at the age of 3 weeks and the neurological damage from that illness prevents her from being able to speak (similar to the plight of some stroke victims). As a result of not being able to verbalize, Samantha expresses herself in odd, unusual sounds, some of which are high-pitched and piercing (similar to a pea-hen or a seagull). Samantha loves her backyard. She signs "play" immediately after breakfast. Unfortunately, (name omitted) who lives behind us and one house to the west of our yard, objects to Samantha's noise. Consequently, he has waged a verbal war with us for years, telling us Samantha has no place in this neighborhood, that she should be institutionalized, or at the very least, locked in her room.

Now I ask you, is this an attitude for a member of a "benevolent and protective order", an organization devoted to helping children? Do you, the members of an organization that has done so much for handicapped children, want a man in your membership who is doing his utmost to keep a handicapped child from using her own yard because her noise annoys him?

I am hereby requesting your help for this one child in the form of a verbal or written reprimand to this man suggesting, instead of trying to "get rid" of Samantha, that he opens his eyes and his heart to her plight and learns to coexist in the same neighborhood with her.

Sincerely,
Suzanne C. Brown
Wife of Alan Herboldsheimer, Member # XXXX"

A short time later we heard that a delegation of Elks had visited our neighbor and that he is no longer a member of the Elks Club. We never heard anything further from our back fence neighbors!

PART THREE

CHAPTER TWENTY SIX;

Her 8th Transfer

<u>September 6, 1988</u>

Samantha has been transferred to yet another campus – her 8th new school. She will attend San Marcos High School. She is also losing another favorite teacher, Beth M.

Samantha attended less than a week before she simply decided enough is enough! I was having to literally drag her out the door and push her onto the bus. She retaliated by biting and scratching her arms until they looked like raw meat from the shoulder to her wrists. I withdrew her from class, took 2 weeks leave of absence from work and stayed home with her. At the end of the two weeks, I gave her one more chance to go back to school. I drove her to the campus instead of sending her on the bus. When we arrived, she refused to get out of the car. I never knew what happened between Sam and the new teacher, but I think I would have endangered her health (mentally and physically) if I had insisted that she go back to class.

I went to Santa Barbara Research Center to consult with the Human Resources Manager and tendered my resignation. I had less than a year and a half to go to be eligible to retire with full benefits. The HR Manager suggested that instead of resigning, I could take early retirement and be eligible for a 5 year payout of funds I had accrued. This sounded OK because I knew Alan would be ready to retire with full benefits before 5 more years.

We had planned to take early retirement at age 55 because Alan was an only child. His father had died of cancer in August and his mother was going to be needing us to help care for her before very much longer.

With my finances taken care of, the next step was to inform the school board and Samantha's caseworker at Tri-Counties Regional Center that Samantha would no longer be attending school. A meeting was held with all parties concerned to discuss this. It turned out that the County School was legally obligated to continue Sammie's schooling until she turned 18. I refused to budge from my position that Samantha's health would be endangered if we forced her to go to school. Finally it was decided that Samantha could be "home-schooled" until her 18th birthday which would occur on April 21, 1989. Kathy H. was appointed case manager/program coordinator. She would monitor Samantha's home schooling and report back to the "interdisciplinary team".

Kathy wrote an Individual Program Plan that we were to follow:

Long Range Goals
1. Maintenance of placement in the community at home
2. Appropriate medical care
3. Appropriate financial income

Objectives and Plans
1. Samantha will have appropriate medical care to include at least an annual physical evaluation.
2. She will have appropriate dental care to include at least an annual dental evaluation.
3. She will have SSI/Medical benefits determined to include rate of benefits at the independent living rate, along with in home supportive services.
4. Samantha will continue to reside in her parent's home. She will have Conservatorship by 4/90.

(When a handicapped child becomes 18 years old, she legally becomes a ward of the state. In order to have control of her and be able to make medical decisions for her, I had to go to court to be declared her Conservator).

5. Samantha will continue to engage in one social/recreational activity per day under her parents supervision. Her parents will determine the type of activity and provide ongoing supervision

for her in order to ensure that participation is achieved in a safe, rewarding manner.

6. Samantha will continue to perform one household task per day involving such activities as putting dishes away, making her bed or setting the table. Samantha's parents will select the household tasks to be performed. They will provide supervision and training as appropriate. They will monitor the completion of the task in order to ensure that it is done in a safe manner.

Samantha and I had a wonderful time with her "home schooling". Alan's boys were grown and gone so our family was just Alan, me, Samantha and Andrea. After Alan left for work and Andrea left for school, Samantha and I cleaned up the kitchen and made the beds which satisfied her "household task" requirement and then had the rest of the day to take care of the social/recreational activity. We lived within walking distance of the beach and Sam loved the ocean. Her skin healed up and all of her bad behaviors that she had displayed at school went away. We traveled to numerous public beaches up and down the coast. When it was lunch time, we bought whatever was available at the little shops at the beach and ate outdoors at the picnic tables. It was a free and easy time for both of us.

When the weather turned cold, we spent more time in the house. Alan had been coming home at noon and preparing his own lunch while we were off exploring beaches. I took over that job and Sammie helped with table setting and clearing up. After lunch she and I worked on her speech.

In November of 1988 another life-changing event took place. SBRC was running low on programs and needed to do some downsizing. Instead of laying people off, they were offering early retirement with full benefits plus a financial bonus (fondly referred to as a Golden Parachute) for anyone who was nearing retirement age. Alan decided to take advantage of their offer and on December 1st, 1988, he retired.

The first thing we decided to do with this new leisure time was to travel to Michigan to visit my family. Andrea had an after school job in a local ice cream shop and didn't want to go with us. She had a close friendship with twin daughters of a neighborhood family, so she opted to stay with them. That left Samantha, Alan and 1 and we meandered North from California to Michigan. Over the years Samantha had become an intrepid traveler and she seemed to enjoy this trip. Although, for reasons we never understood, when we stayed overnight in the motels she began sleeping in the bathtubs! The first couple of nights we tucked her into her bed and while we were sleeping, she would go sleep in the tub. Once we realized what she was doing, we put pillows and blankets into the tub so she would be more comfortable. We also searched out motels with indoor swimming pools in order to satisfy Sam's need for exercise. The farther North we got, the more snow and ice we ran into.

When we arrived in Michigan, we spent our days at my sister and brother-in-law's home and in the evening we checked into a motel nearby that had a large indoor swimming pool. Samantha enjoyed playing outdoors in the snow, although she wouldn't keep her mittens on so we didn't let her stay out very long at a time. I got to visit with my entire family and they were delighted with the progress Samantha had made since the last time they had seen her. The day we left there was a blizzard with ice and snow on the roads and "lake effect" snow blowing in the wind. The tires on our van never touched a clear road until we got to Indiana!

April 21, 1989 : Samantha's 18th Birthday
Our first order of business was to start the proceedings for Conservator. We consulted our attorney and he began drawing up the petition for the court hearing.

To the Superior Court of California, County of Santa Barbara: Notice is given that Suzanne C. Brown has filed Petition for Appointment of Conservator of the Person of Samantha Jo Brown, conservatee.

The proposed Conservatee is substantially handicapped due to autism. She is functionally non verbal. Although she does understand some signs and uses them occasionally, it is difficult for individuals not familiar with her signs to understand what she is saying. Verbally she uses approximately 10 half syllables which are understood only by her parents and close family members.

A copy of a letter from Lee N. of Tri Counties Regional Center dated June, 1989 is attached for further particulars.

"Samantha Brown, who has been a client of Tri-Counties Regional Center since March 20, 1976, resides at the home of her mother and stepfather. She is eligible for

TCRC services as she is substantially handicapped due to autism. Samantha has been receiving Supplemental Security Income benefits since her 18th birthday in April of this year. Although eligible for Special Education Services from the County School system until she is 21 years of age, the mother withdrew her from school programming in November of 1988 because in the fall of this last school year Samantha experienced a severe shutdown of her basic care skills (she stopped eating, became dehydrated, and began having bowel and bladder accidents) and engaged in constant self-abuse (scratching and biting her body severely). Her mother felt that it was a reaction to her inability to handle the pressure in expectations of a program away from her home environment. Samantha withdrew, refused to eat, was in danger of becoming dehydrated. Feeling that her behavior was a response to her inability to deal with stress, her mother, who was employed on a full-time basis at the time, remained home from work keeping Samantha out of school for a two-week period. At the end of the two-week period, Mrs. Brown was noting an improvement in Samantha's coping behaviors, increased interest in eating, and increased interest in complying with the activities of daily living. She determined that it was necessary for her to take early retirement so that she could care for Samantha. This was accomplished at the end of 1988. Following Samantha's 18th birthday in April of 1989, Samantha was officially withdrawn from school by her mother.

Samantha's ongoing medical care is provided by Dr. Joseph S. of the Santa Barbara Medical Foundation Clinic. Although Mrs. Brown is aware that Samantha is eligible for MediCal, she has elected to use Dr. S. and fund her medical care through the parents' medical insurance. She is aware that Santa Barbara Medical Foundation Clinic does not accept MediCal patients.

Medically, for the past few years, Samantha has not presented with medical problems. She does not take any ongoing medication. Since Dr. S. has had some experience with Samantha, Mrs. Brown feels comfortable with continuing this relationship for the present. For the same reason, Mrs. Brown had continued to have Samantha seen by Dr. L., a pediatric dentist. He also does not take MediCal, but has had considerable experience with Samantha and has elected to continue to see her for the present despite the behavioral problems with which she presents when dental care is necessary.

In her current setting, it is necessary for Mrs. Brown to supervise Samantha at all times. It has been necessary for them to adapt their home in order to ensure, for example, that Samantha does not open the front door and leave the house without Mrs. Brown's knowledge. Samantha is functionally non verbal. Although she does understand some signs and uses them occasionally, when motivated to do so, it is difficult for individuals not familiar with Samantha's signs to understand what she is saying as she has adapted standard signs to suit her own needs. Samantha has resumed liking to go for walks, and going to the beach. Her mother is able to take her for short selected trips to the stores and Samantha is given the opportunity to decide if she wants to go or not. If she is feeling stressed or frustrated, she engages in loud noise-making behavior which makes it difficult to handle her in the community. It is necessary for Mrs. Brown to be completely responsible for all of Samantha's care.

As you can see, this young woman definitely needs protective supervision. I hope this information will be sufficient to enable you to plan this status for her. If services were not available in her current setting, it is highly probable that this young woman would be placed in a State Hospital program due to the severe nature of her disability."

<u>June 15, 1989</u>: A letter to Dr. S. from me

"Dear Dr. S.: The last time that you saw Samantha Brown was because she had "shut down", stopped eating, stopped cooperating, started a routine of constant self-abuse. I had taken a leave-of-absence from my work at SBRC in order to stay home with her. After a week she had seemed calmer and I had tried to send her back to school. She refused to go and the self-injurious behavior began again. At that time, I made arrangements to take "early retirement" from SBRC and stay home to take care of Samantha.

I did not fill the anti-depressant prescription you gave us, but instead I removed all the pressure from Samantha's life. I made absolutely no demands; I treated her as a physically ill person; I kept her calm with a great deal of water therapy – several baths each day in a full tub of hot water with bubble-bath; several times a day in the spa with the whirlpool jets turned on. Her response was gratifying. Within a few weeks (with the help of the Silvadene cream you prescribed) her skin scabbed over and healed up. Her weight returned to normal and her attitude also returned to normal.

Because Samantha has turned 18 years old and I no longer have the right to order medical treatment for her, I am applying for conservatorship . My attorney will request a letter from you verifying that it is necessary for me to strictly supervise Samantha in order to keep her from harming herself.

If you would like to have me bring Samantha to your office to discuss this, we could do so. If you feel you could just write the letter without an office visit, please do so."

<u>June 28, 1989</u> : A letter from our attorney to Dr. S.

"Dear Dr. S.: Mrs. Suzanne C. Brown, natural mother of Samantha Jo Brown, has requested that I prepare for filing a Petition for Appointment for Conservator seeking to have Suzanne C. Brown appointed conservator of the person of Samantha Jo. Brown. She advises that you are Samantha's treating physician.

Enclosed please find Declaration of Medical or Accredited Practitioner. Please review, complete the same, execute on the line indicated for your signature and then return to me in the enclosed self-addressed envelope at your early convenience.

I am informed that Samantha Jo Brown is unable to attend a court hearing seeking appointment of a conservator because of medical inability. Please set forth her medical condition and inability either by typing directly onto the enclosed form or by preparing a separate letter which can be attached to the Declaration.

Your prompt attention and cooperation is appreciated. If you have any questions, please feel free to contact me.

Kindest regards,
K. F., Attorney at Law

With the cooperation and assistance of the people who sent letters to the attorney confirming Samantha's disability, the conservatorship was approved by the Superior Court. On September 29, 1989, I received the notice of my appointment:

Letter of Conservatorship Affirmation: I solemnly affirm that I will perform the duties of conservator of Samantha Jo Brown, conservatee. Executed on September 20, 1989 and Filed in Superior Court on October 19, 1989.

After that the next order of business for us was to get our house spiffed up and put up for sale (new roof, new carpet, new paint). When Alan's Dad retired, they had sold their house in San Francisco and relocated to Cambria, California, where they bought a beautiful 2-story home right on the bluff above the Pacific Ocean. The upper story was a rental unit. We had assumed that we would move into it when the folks decided they needed our help. Alan's Mom, who was in her mid-80's, and had a large circle of women friends in the neighborhood, decided she didn't need us. She did admit that it would be nice if we found something nearby. Her decision gave me a huge sense of relief! Now we were free to begin looking for a ranch!

We talked to a realtor in Cambria, told him our requirements, and he informed us that ranches in that area were few and far between and out of our price range. He referred us to a realtor in Paso Robles. There is a mountain range between the ocean and Paso Robles. It is a beautiful 45 minute drive between Cambria and Paso Robles. Not too close and not too far from Alan's Mom. We loved the small-town feel of the town as soon as we saw it and the realtor we found was certain that she could find exactly what we were looking for. We wanted enough land so that we could have horses and dogs and we wanted it isolated enough so that Samantha would not disturb any neighbors with her noise.

We spent several weekends looking at properties East of the town of Paso Robles. The realtor, Kathy, was very patient with us as we toured the area with Samantha and two Siberian Huskies. Finally, just about the time that our house was sold, she brought us down Hog Canyon Road to Independence Ranch. This was a 1200 acre ranch that had been parceled into 10 to 20 acre ranchettes. It had gravel roads and rolling hills and, best of all, a small new house that sat up on a hill and faced the mountain range to the west. The minute we saw it, we knew it was The One for us. It has 7 acres rather than 10 because a corner of it had been split off and sold, but that was big enough for us and the price was right.

In November of 1990, it was impressed upon us that our daughter was now a ward of the State of California, when a Court Investigator showed up on our doorstep.

THE SUPERIOR COURT OF THE STATE OF CALIFORNIA FOR THE COUNTY OF SANTA BARBARA

COURT INVESTIGATOR'S REVIEW REPORT
In the Matter of the Conservatorship of Samantha Jo Brown, Conservatee
Conservator of Person: Suzanne C. Brown
Attorney for Conservator: K. F.

Date of Interview: November 2, 1990
Place of Interview: Conservatee's residence, Anchor Drive, Goleta CA.
Age of Conservatee: Nineteen years

Requirements: The conservatee was not informed of the facts relating to her conservatorship as she is handicapped due to autism. The conservatee is nonverbal and is unlikely to comprehend an explanation of the conservatorship. The conservatee continues to reside in the home of her mother (the conservator), and stepfather. The conservatee's needs are being appropriately met by the conservator.

Opinion Regarding Continuing Need for Conservatorship: The conservatee is clearly in need of the continuation of this conservatorship due to her autism. The conservatee is dependent upon her mother and stepfather for the majority of her daily needs and is unable to function in an independent living environment.

The conservator indicated to this investigator that the family has sold their residence and it is their intention to move to Paso Robles, California.

The conservator indicated to this investigator that the family had decided to make this move due to problems they had experienced from a neighbor in the past few years. Their new residence will be in a rural area and will afford them the privacy they feel they need in order to continue to have the conservatee in their care.

It is believed that the family decision regarding the move to Paso Robles would probably be in the bests interests of this family.

Respectfully submitted,
Susan G
Chief Probation Officer

On December 7, 1990, we bid goodbye to our friends in Goleta and moved the 120 miles North to Paso Robles. At the last minute our youngest daughter, Andrea, decided to come with us even though we were 10 miles outside of town and she wasn't crazy about the idea of such a rural area. Samantha loved the new place! She spent the first few days going in and out of all the doors, feeling a freedom she had not felt in the small backyard in Goleta.

On December 23rd, 1990, the temperature dropped overnight to 9 degrees, a historic low, and our well pump froze. We found that we had a lot to learn about living in the country! First, we called the company that had drilled the well and they came out and replaced the pump. Then, Alan traveled to several places in Paso Robles looking for electric heat tapes that could be attached to the well pipes, but, because this was a very unusual event and a lot of people had burst water pipes and other problems, there had been a run on that type of supplies and he had to drive 70 miles South to Santa Maria. He attached the heat tapes that evening and the following day he built a small shed around the well pipes.

Shortly after that, the winter rains started and our driveway, which was composed of adobe clay, turned to mud and our vehicles sank into huge ruts. Andrea owned a Volkswagon and hers got stuck (maybe just from lack of driving experience). We called a local contractor who came out with two huge trailers full of gravel that he poured into our sea of mud. He then used a huge grader to smooth it out and our driveway was useable once again. However, between Samantha and the 2 Siberian Huskies, large amounts of mud were tracked into the house throughout that first winter.

In the Spring, we hired a neighbor with a tractor to drill post holes and then built a wooden fence around 5 acres of the ranch. Next came another contractor who put up three covered stalls and we began to look for the horses to fill them. First came a young gelding named John Henry (after a famous racehorse of the same name). He had quite a bit of Arabian blood and was a beautiful chestnut color. Then we found a big bay mare named Bear-ly Made It. Her name came about because she had just enough white spots to make it into the Paint Horse registry.

Alan and I built a big, sturdy swing for Samantha. It was constructed out of 10 foot tall 4x4's and we attached a wooden swing that had a bench seat, a back and arms. We added pads that made it very comfortable for her. She loved it and spent so much time swinging on it that we had to change out the hardware because she was wearing it out. We also found inexpensive radios that we tied to the swing so that she could play them. When she wore out the batteries, she would take Alan by the hand and show him her "dead" radio.

Sam's Entertainment Center

We tried to get Samantha to ride the bay mare, Bear, but it didn't work out very well. Sammie would get into the saddle and pick up the reins and I would get on John Henry, but when we started out, Bear would turn around and take Sam back to the hitching rail. We think she understood that Sam had a problem and was trying to keep her safe. At any rate, the only way it worked out was with me getting off my horse and leading Bear around. Not quite the scenario we had in mind of riding off over the hills together!

We quickly realized that we needed a tractor in order to take care of our property. Alan's Mom told him to look for one and she would buy it for him for his birthday in April. She was very happy about our decision to get this property and often brought friends of hers over to have lunch with us and admire our progress. There were several tractor dealers in the area and Alan finally chose a medium-size Kubota that had a front-loader that operated hydraulically and a Power Take-Off in the rear that could be used to attach equipment like mowers and rototillers. The Operator's Manual had page after page of safety instructions! Alan had a lot to learn. Because his mother had made the initial investment, we were able to start buying other necessary equipment. I was anxious to start a large vegetable garden, so the rototiller came first.

After Alan rototilled a large area, I planted a hundred tomato plants, several rows of sweet corn, peas and zucchini. I was a farm kid all of my growing up years and I was ecstatically happy to spend part of every day taking care of this garden. It grew an abundant crop that first year and I was thrilled to be able to not only use the vegetables throughout the summer, but also can and freeze what we didn't eat.

We settled into a routine of starting our day at 5 am, having a large breakfast, then feeding the horses and dogs. Samantha joined us and helped carry the feed. After that we all took our two Siberian Huskies for a walk up and down the rolling hills on the property. One morning we were walking up our driveway when one of the huskies, who was on a long lead rope, jumped off to the side into some long grass. She reached down and grabbed a snake and tossed it up in the air! Andrea, who had been complaining about being too tired to walk up the hill, took off like an Olympian runner and made it to the top in record time!

Rattlesnakes have not been a big problem on the ranch, but we worried that Samantha was vulnerable because she would not recognize the danger. We bought cowboy boots to give her some protection and kept vegetation cut down so she wouldn't be walking in tall grass.

There were a lot of small rocks on the property, mostly less than golf-ball size, and Samantha found a new pastime. She had a great throwing arm! Suddenly all the flat places on our buildings were becoming covered with rocks and several windows were broken in the process. Alan built heavy duty screens to cover the windows in the house and his 2-story barn. He also nailed a garbage can cover on the wall of our carport and tried to teach her to use it as a target. We had to be careful to keep our trucks in the carport after she broke a windshield. Worst of all, one time when Karen (my oldest daughter) and her husband parked in our driveway, she chucked a rock through a side window on their SUV!

Samantha's behavior had been exceptionally good since our move to the ranch (aside from the rock-throwing, of course), but then in 1992 Andrea decided to move back to the Goleta/Santa Barbara area. She had really never been happy living so far out in such a rural area and she missed the friends she had grown up with. Her departure threw Samantha into a depression and she stopped eating and started her old self-abuse behaviors. We realized that she didn't understand why her sister was no longer with us, so we took her to Goleta and spent the day with Andrea. She literally howled the whole 135 miles down to Goleta, but on the way back, she was quiet. She understood.

On November 17, 1992, I received the following letter from the Probation Department, County of Santa Barbara:

RE: Conservatorship of Samantha Jo Brown

"According to our records, the last investigation of this conservatorship was completed and approved on October 9, 1990.

Pursuant to the provision of Probate Code Section 1850, which requires a review one year after its establishment and biennially thereafter, an appropriate review of this conservatorship is due at this time.

Please contact me as soon as possible in order to assist me in filing the appropriate report with the Court.

Donna L., Court Investigator"

I telephoned her and she agreed to allow me to take care of the matter by writing a letter.

"Donna L., Court Investigator
Re: Conservatorship of Samantha J. Brown

In accordance with our telephone conversation of yesterday, this is my report of Samantha's lifestyle since your last investigation.

In December 1990, we moved from Anchor Drive in Goleta to our present address in San Miguel (as proposed in our original request for conservatorship). We have 7 acres of land with a small ranch house, barn, and horse corral. All of the land around us is divided into 7 to 20 acre plots, so there are no neighbors near enough to be disturbed by Samantha's screeching noises. As you can see in her file, this was a big problem in Goleta. It is wonderful to be able to let her play outdoors whenever she wants without worrying about her noise.

The second big benefit for Samantha in our move is that she now goes about freely, in or out of any door she chooses, whereas in Goleta she was restricted to the small, fenced-in backyard due to her lack of understanding about street traffic. We now live on a country gravel road and are far enough away from it that she never goes near it except when she accompanies us on walks.

Samantha's general health is excellent, although she went through a 3-month emotional shut-down when her younger sister, Andrea moved away to begin her adult life separately from us. She and Samantha have always been very, very close and Samantha took a long time to adjust to her absence. She stopped eating and started biting, scratching and bruising herself, as she does in stressful situations. We took her to Dr. S. in Templeton three times during this period of time. He prescribed a salve that was helpful in healing her scratches and advised us to give her the liquid protein Ensure to maintain her body during her self-imposed fasting. She recovered and started eating again in October and has regained 10 of the 20 pounds she lost.

There has, of course, been no change in her condition and she is 95% dependent upon us for all of her needs. She was recently reviewed by the San Luis Obispo County Department of Social Services. Her service worker in that office is Bill R. and his telephone number is 805-XXX-XXXX.

If further information is needed, please contact us.

Sincerely,
Suzanne C. Brown, Mother of Samantha Brown
and Alan F. Herboldsheimer, Stepfather of Samantha Brown"

We now have three State Officials checking up on us annually or biannually – the Superior Court for the County of Santa Barbara, the San Luis Obispo County Department of Social Services, and the In-Home-Support-Service of San Luis Obispo. It is actually comforting to know that these individuals are checking up on Sammie and know that we are taking good care of her.

EPILOGUE

As a family, we have been able to enjoy much of what Paso Robles has to offer. Samantha has enjoyed the various parades, air shows, movies and restaurants in town. We were so fortunate to be able to find an area that is the least restrictive place for her. Early retirement has meant we have had our day in the sun while we were young and healthy enough to enjoy it all.

Late in 2005 and early 2006 there were several changes in our lives. One of these began shortly after Christmas 1995. Samantha suddenly began to sleep almost 95% of the time. In her bed, in her chair, at the table, in the truck – she could not stay awake. We took her to our family doctor and he began looking for the cause. All of her physical tests were in the normal range; he could find nothing significantly wrong. He finally sent us to a neurologist who ordered an MRI. The MRI shows ongoing deterioration of Samantha's brain. The diagnosis: early-onset dementia. Further research on the internet shows that when one has suffered profound brain damage as a result of encephalitis, it is not unusual for the symptoms Samantha has experienced to return in later years. She has lost the sight in her right eye due to an inoperable cataract. She has also lost almost all of the verbal skill she had gained. Now, instead of getting up early and running outdoors to play, she goes to bed early in the evening and sleeps in until 9:30 or 10 in the morning. She goes out for short periods of time and then goes back and lies down.

Years ago we were told she would have a normal life-span. Now we are less confident of that. She is approaching her 40th birthday and we have no idea what the future will bring for her. What we do know is that we have been blessed with her presence in our lives. We love her more dearly than words can tell. She is our beautiful, loving, funny forever-child.

GLOSSARY

1. gravida-a pregnant woman

2. lateral ventricle of brain: one cavity of a system of 4 communicating cavities within the brain

3. nystagmus – involuntary eye movement

4. propioceptive: a sensory receptor found in muscles, tendons, joints and the inner ear, that detects motion

5. temporal horn: lateral ventricle of brain (see 2 above)

6. Stim, stimming – self-stimulation

7. Vestibular: the middle cavity of the inner ear

ILLUSTRATIONS

Picture 1. Sammie trying to get Andrea's attention

Picture 2. Meeting Alan's parents

Pictures 3., 4., 5. Horseback riding lessons

Picture 6. Sammie. Fall of 1981

Picture 7. Sammie. Fall of 1982

Picture 8. Arriving at Yellowstone National Park, Wyoming

Picture 9. Yellowstone National Park, Wyoming

Picture 10. Mid Southern Nebraska

Picture 11. Northern Michigan